IN THE DOORWAY

IN THE DOORWAY

---
a memoir

---

by

LINDA GRAVENSON

International Psychoanalytic Books
New York • http://www.IPBooks.net

Published by IPBooks, Queens, NY
Online at: www.IPBooks.net

Cover Design by Blackthorn Studio
Typesetting by Noel S. Morado

ISBN: 978-1-956864-71-7

For Nick and Bexon

1

"I'm dying and they bring me mashed potatoes!" My mother shrieked, slamming her fist on the hospital tray, sitting straight up in bed, a flowered scarf tied rakishly around her hair, her lipstick a fuchsia slash, her eyes as roving, as wild as other times she has been this manic. She was in the middle of her aria and the usual mania, background to the foreground of another medical emergency now that congestive heart disease was taking center stage.

I stood in the doorway as she stabbed at the air with her index finger, commanding me to take my seat for the performance. Suddenly hoarse, she croaked, "Sons of bitches! Twerps!"

I was there because my husband, Eckart, drove me to Manhattan and delivered me, like a package. I hadn't been able to leave our block in Brooklyn, on my own, for years. I'd kept this from her because she'd have dismissed the news, sailing over the information, back to the ever-running movie she starred in.

How this frail, mad woman was holding court in the intensive-care cardiac unit speaks of her sheer force. It was the early Seventies, years before manic-depression will be called *bipolar disorder* and when psychotropic cocktails were more of a potshot than a bull's eye. Wild as wind again, she muttered insults as the nurses adjusted her tubes and changed the catheter in her neck. She had them jumping as her thoughts leaped, dipped, and dived. Although she waved me closer, I didn't move.

Smiling dreamily, like her *doppelgänger,* the 1940s screen star Mary Astor, she called out, "The doorman, the doorman. Sailing on the *Liberté*. Middle of the movie. Mad money. Wrapped in wildflowers." *Wrapped in wildflowers* is how she'd described, after one of the many electroshock treatments at the Westchester sanatorium, coming home from a childhood picnic with her mother. Was my mother wrapped in wildflowers or was it the grandmother whom I never knew, who will die of diabetes when my mother is fifteen? Or was my mother telling me something about herself? Bea was the sixth child of a diabetic woman who'd been warned of having more babies. When I was in college, *wrapped in wildflowers* would come back to me, when my father insisted I return to Manhattan to help him, to ride in an ambulance with her, like today when she was wild as wind.

The smile gone, she growled, "You! Teddy's daughter! That salesman. Your father! You! That Sarah Lawrence girl, you! Middle of the movie!" As a little girl, I was told so-and-so was "in the middle of the movie" when I longed for regular connections, wanted her to be regular. *I* was in the middle of the movie, she'd hiss, a movie only she could see.

Eyes flashing, she beckoned me closer, calling out for all to hear: "They gave me the wrong baby, the wrong baby after my Caesarean!" Surely I have misheard. I stepped closer to the bed and leaned towards her as she sang out triumphantly, operatically, "The wrong baby!" Her eyes met mine for one of the few times I will remember.

For twenty years, in or out of the hospital, medicated or on the loose in Manhattan, we were entangled. I ricocheted between revulsion and attachment, hoping, despite her diagnosis, she might return to me, spunky but not crazy, even playful—the wacky, sometimes tender Mom of my Greenwich Village childhood.

As always, her words found their mark, but these were even closer to the knot of our story. As a child and then a teen, as her outbursts became more and more threatening, I'd fantasized that she wasn't my real mother, but because I needed to be somebody's daughter, I kept coming back. And now, as a young mother, I was loyal, crazy in my own way.

She settled back against the pillows, closing her eyes for a brief intermission. I scanned the unit, hoping no one else had heard. Tethered by a web of IVs, she couldn't leap from the sheets, but I backed away from the bed, trembling, keeping in view the snarling dog. Her once beautiful fingers were more like claws, the polish peeling, the nails ragged, but still able to pierce if she clutched my wrist—or like that one time, after graduation, before I moved out, when my father had just left, when she'd put her hands around my throat, digging in with those shiny nails.

Even as I saw her tethered by the ravages of twenty years of madness, not just by the tangle of IVs, she had me on high alert—where I've been as long as I can remember. I whispered to her closed eyes, "Mom, I have to go now. Eckart's waiting in the car."

Eyes open, IV tube swinging, she bellowed again, "Fat ass! Get that Jewish ass out of here!" We are, both of us, Jewish. No matter how many times (or how slim I am) her words punched. My temples throbbed, my tongue thickened. Once again I was speechless, in a freeze frame, as she stared at the ceiling, crooning, "You are my lifeline." Not her sunshine, her only sunshine. The wrong baby was her lifeline.

My cheeks burned, and my eyes filled as I waited for the elevator—dreading its emptiness, and even more, dreading that it might be crowded. My palms were damp. My old gregarious, even flirtatious, self had disappeared. In its place is someone in hiding.... *Get to the car! Get inside to Eckart*, who, despite his growing coldness and remoteness, still offered protection from this woman who had just declared me... a mistake.

As I slipped in beside him, he stared straight ahead, jaw set, his profile as fierce as it could be, to deliver me back to Second Place in Carroll Gardens to our dilapidated half-renovated brownstone, to our beautiful little boy. We crossed the Brooklyn Bridge in silence, as I asked myself yet again, *if not all alcoholics are mean drunks, are all manic depressives as mean as my mother can be? Was this crazy talk just her? Or was it the illness?*

After supper, with Nico asleep, I told Eckart what she'd said, leaving out the slam about my ass. Later, on opposite sides of our bed, what had become my good-night question came flooding back. Is this how he dealt with the disappearance of the adventuresome young journalist he'd been assigned to guide in West Berlin, where he'd been, the eternal *student* just managing on an interpreter's salary in the government Press Office? I'd been daring, taken risks. A young woman who lay down with well-known writers, as if in apprenticeship, who flew headlong into escapades, who was now grounded, silently counting steps, to make it from here to there.

2

I was swallowing to be sure I still could. The brownstones opposite ours were bathed in late-afternoon, fall sunlight. Somehow, a few days a week, I made it across our street (which might as well have been the Hudson River) to pick up three-year-old Nico from his play group. Even without checking my watch, the light told me it was the time to open the front door, to hold my breath, to count the steps of the stoop, and to slip past the gate at the end of our bluestone walk.

I wiped my clammy palms against my jeans before gripping the door knob, as if it were a diving board. The knob was etched brass, one of the few remaining original details in our 1865 brownstone, giving the wrong impression of what you would find here. This was never a Henry James brownstone, and I was not the Heiress. Two years into panic attacks and phobia, this dilapidated building was my haven and my prison. I was a thirty-three-year-old mother, frozen in her doorway, in a kind of self-imposed house arrest, waiting for a spell to lift—as if someone else had created it. Letting go of the knob, I checked myself in the long Pier mirror. It had become a habit to check and recheck my reflection to see if it was me, unable to open the door, standing under a large paper lantern, like the one in my first post-college apartment, when a Japanese lantern was my moon, hung with pleasure and bravado, when I'd had my first job as a fact checker at *Esquire* and could never have imagined a time when errands would turn a peaceful Brooklyn neighborhood into mine fields. A still youngish woman stared back from the mirror. My dark hair touched my shoulders, no longer the blunt cut needing frequent trips to a hairdresser. Stamps cost three cents more than when I stopped going out alone, stopped taking Nico on outings without a *safe* person, stopped needing a shoemaker for repairs, began ordering from catalogs to avoid a panic attack in a shop, and like a Victorian neurasthenic, started to carry smelling salts to ward off another blackout.

I took a Mexican shawl from the coat rack and swung it across my shoulders, as I did when I'd sailed out on a date or to work as a journalist in New York and in West Berlin, centuries ago. My summer uniform of black cotton had changed now that curled brown leaves lined the curbs. Peering through the glass, I willed the block to be empty. I'd given all my neighbors x-ray vision. They must know I'm in hiding and can barely meet their gaze. How could I have become this pathetic creature when I was blessed with my darling boy? As sweat broke out beneath my collar, the phone rang. Although it could be another of my mother's manic rants, I might answer. Anything was easier than opening the glass-paned door to the air, being *outside,* being *seen,* imagining a free-fall to the bottom of the stoop. Counting the steps was how I could trick myself, how I wouldn't fall. As usual there were three rings before she slammed the phone back onto its cradle.

My blouse stuck to my back, my temples were pounding. I hung the shawl back on the peg and returned to the kitchen. Fierce determination to stay inside overrode any scrap of dignity left in me.

One more time, 1 will call my neighbor Evie to ask if she can bring Nico home.

"It's no big deal," she said lightly, "in a few minutes.

Does she sense how humiliated I am when I can't leave my house, just to cross our street, which has become a river of a street? Inexplicable shame hangs on me, a mysterious cloak I can't explain to anyone. Did she sense that I was in the grip of waves of nausea, flaming cheeks, throbbing temples, as if a mysterious virus had taken up residence and could spring into action without warning? Is she mystified by my requests even though, by now, she knows I avoid wide-open spaces, crowds, going anywhere without a safe person? Eckart, was no longer designated, as agoraphobics do, my *safe* person. But unable to imagine life without him, the protection he provided from my mother, and lacking the trust funds of my college friends, I made allowances for his cool distancing, especially after we'd made love which, as a Fifties girl, I didn't describe as having sex.

That afternoon I knew Evie was dying to watch her soaps with her son, Josh, munching Cheese Doodles on the velvet sofa she and her husband had just restored. Their renovation showed ambition and resolve, a couple pulling together instead of our half-finished project; ceilings still festooned with electric cable, gaping holes of lath and plaster. Even if stalled renovations don't have the power to change lives, they do shine a merciless light—evidence that Eckart and I weren't up for the job and should never have taken on a four-story brownstone coming down around our heels in 1969, twenty years before Carroll Gardens will become one of Brooklyn's hot spots, before the *cognoscenti* will have turned the Mom and Pop stores into corner cafes.

Our front parlor overlooked the patch of pachysandra I planted in 1970, that first spring of Nico's life, when crouched in moist dirt, digging deep to root the seedlings, I was still buoyant with hormones and not anticipating a slide into postpartum darkness. The plants took, and after the next winter resumed their gloss. Now they reminded me I was still a prisoner on my own block.

I spent too much time at our parlor windows or on the stoop, memorizing the view: over the garden gate and east to Court Street, where I used to market or walked up Clinton to cross Atlantic Avenue back and forth to the Heights—to civilization. As I watched Nico playing with the other kids, I was teary, imagining their mothers on Court Street, *regular* mothers chatting as they ambled home with their kids. Because the Court Street butcher and the greengrocer delivered, Carroll Gardens accommodated an agoraphobic who couldn't imagine walking the mile to Atlantic Avenue ever again, crossing that wide space with her son, walking back to the Heights, to a time when she'd been a young woman taking risks—such as marrying her German boyfriend from West Berlin.

The neighborhood wives lean on their window sills for hours with pillows, cushioning their elbows. Most of the women leave their houses on their own, but others only with a friend or family member escorting them to church or on an errand. As I watched them walking arm-in-arm down our block, I longed to slip into these families, imagined being magically transported to households where my mortifying panic attacks would be overlooked, where it's not big news for a grown woman to go out only with her sister, her aunt, or her mother, where being house-bound, block-bound is no big deal and won't bring the shame I felt every day. Did the UPS man see in a flash that I wasn't in charge and ask if the lady of the house is at home? Or that she was ambushed by panic attacks that have escalated to agoraphobia and can't begin to describe the terror of an ordinary day? All this, plus x-ray vision, I gave to the unsuspecting UPS man.

Trapped in this corner of South Brooklyn, two psychiatrists had failed to get me around the block on my own. What transforms trauma into hard-bound phobia? Each of us has an album from which to choose. We humans are remarkably creative and can construct boundaries that will keep us tied. *Ties that bind* can mean family, marriage, enduring friendship but the darker side is entangled knots— safety at any cost.

Other than my crazy mother in Manhattan, we had no family nearby. Eckart's father had been a reserve officer in Hitler's army, and was killed in 1939 when Germany invaded Poland, calling it a "police action." His widowed mother was still living in Bavaria, and my father (the un-crazy parent) and stepmother had retired to their new life in Mexico when Nico was a few months old. I had been so used to keeping distance from my mother that I didn't realize, when I became a Mom, that I longed for a Mother even if I couldn't long for *her*, but longed for who she'd been before midnight ambulance rides, shock treatments—the good-enough Mother.

Today, instead of being relieved she was nowhere in sight, I imagined her beside me in the hall mirror, lost in one of the catatonic depressions that punctuated her manic swings, peering into her gold compact, not applying powder or lipstick, blankly staring like when I was fourteen and tempted to put my arms around her frozen stillness when she was subdued, more a pale line drawing than a kaleidoscope of color racing full speed at me. My father was still in that picture, still able to sell me the Brooklyn Bridge with his wide smile, eyes as dark as mine, and what I will learn in first-year French—his *joie de vivre.*

The phone rang again. My hand went to my throat. What might I say if I wasn't trying to keep her from getting even more manic than she's been all day? Might I try to get her to pay attention to what's happened to me these last two years?

"It's not a good time…" I was imitating a social worker's tone like those who've tried in vain to help when she's been *outside*, not *inside* mental hospitals.

Her furious broken voice, like static (thanks to Thorazine for psychosis), invaded my kitchen: "Middle of the movie! Always too busy! I used to be busy too, my dearest daughter," she hissed, sending her fury, her ragged face through the phone. "They're watching, those bastards… they think I don't know." She's sure the apartment directly across 72nd Street is inhabited by gangsters, ready to rub her out. As she raced on, nearly breathless, I saw the studio where she'd lived for ten years: every surface crowded with half-opened cracker boxes, uncapped lipsticks, a single glove, insurance premiums awaiting a check and a stamp on an envelope tucked deep in the debris—as well as her amazing paintings covering every inch of wall space. Paintings she could no longer create.

I imagined her half-dressed, slamming the receiver down only to redial anyone who would take her call. Friends had vanished years ago. At her worst, she'd take her trash to the garbage disposal in the public hallway, her bathrobe barely covering her nakedness; at her best, she'd wear one of her good tweed jackets and hold one glove in hand as she pressed the elevator button.

For days and today, she'd been threatening to come to Brooklyn to see her grandson. Her grandson!

"Mom, I've got to go . . . Nico's waiting." I lied.

I said "Mom" as in Mom and Apple Pie. *My Mom* whom I craved because when I was two, three, or even four, were there moments of a soft mother paying attention? Or did I make that up, to have her in some way, to be somebody's daughter, even in a false memory? Mysteriously (or so it seemed) I needed her when I was in so much trouble.

"The super won't answer his phone!" she growled, determined to ensnare me.

"He will report you to the building people," I said firmly, although I knew better than to remind her of rules and regulations, of the consequences of breaking them, of those years of midnight ambulance rides and sometimes the police. Bellevue.

Safe in my kitchen, I was feeling careless enough to tell the truth. Suddenly I wanted her to know that on days like this, I can't get out the door and that I count the steps and that getting across the street to Evie's kitchen was fording a river. But my daring fades. I lied again, "I'll call back after I get Nico."

A few days later, with home health-aides doing their best and worst, I interrupted another of her phone rants to ask who is on duty. I needed to know she wasn't roaming the hallways of her building.

"How should I know? There's a Zulu in the kitchen!" She slammed down the receiver leaving me to imagine how, after a twelve-hour shift, the two women have exhausted each other. Long suffering Daisy, her Jamaican aide, will soon head for the depths of Brooklyn to cook for her own family. There's a chance she hadn't heard this loony talk, or if she has, was on to my mother and chalked it up to whatever makes her client not right in the head—images running wild, concocting a Zulu warrior in full war paint washing her lettuce. I left her to her Zulu, grateful it was time again, to be *inside* making supper, chopping and grating with dedication—another day mercifully over.

3

Warm wind brings a baby... when I was pregnant I collected folklore to carry me along this unknown path. Hormones were in high gear—as if I'd been airbrushed with an entirely new palate, colors of confidence. In the first three months, I loved the secret I was holding, and even after we spread the news, l felt privacy between me and my baby. Just as it swam in a protective sack, I too felt protected. Worry vanished so completely that I couldn't recall its ever-present shadow that I'd lived with since childhood or its full-blown residence ever since my mother's first hospitalization for shock treatments during my freshman year at Sarah Lawrence.

After the first few weeks of morning sickness, I emerged from our apartment in Brooklyn Heights with a more confident stride than I'd ever had. And yes, I glowed. Fiercely protective of my baby, a self-preserving instinct was in full bloom. Even though Eckart was with me in the crowded subway car, I held my arm across my belly, on my way to my editorial job at Fawcett Publications on West 44th Street. These days, nothing was allowed to disturb *us*. When my mother had been frozen in depression, I'd often tried, without success, for a response—my arm round her shoulder, my hand on hers. Now when she sat in a chair, her hands in her lap, her gaze blank, I stayed away from her, the visits short. No arm round her shoulder. After years of regret and guilt for keeping my emotional distance, I allowed myself that space. I was protecting what was more than me.

Eckart praised my growing belly, declared it even sexy, and took my hand more than usual when we crossed the city streets, as he had in West Berlin. It was to be our best time. Perhaps inspired by his impending fatherhood, he spoke of his childhood in sudden outbursts,

"When the returnees marched through our village in '45, I was eight, always in the front row, sometimes with my brother but sometimes just alone, watching their faces. I looked so hard at these poor soldiers, searching for *mein Vater*." He didn't notice when German overtook his English and, in this case, I didn't remind him.

His missing father endeared him to me. We were both missing a parent. My mother had been missing from my life for years, if not forever, and his *Vater wurde getötet* in the woods where Polish cadets, unaware of the surrender to Germany, had fired on his tank. His father was buried in Poland and would not be amongst those weary, returning men. Yet he had searched their faces as they marched through the village, either because he didn't believe what he'd been told or wanted to prove them wrong.

Our move from familiar Brooklyn Heights to a dilapidated brownstone below Atlantic Avenue was taken on by a couple of babes. We knew nothing about renovation and had no capital. My father gave us the down payment of $6,000 which had accrued from some bonds bought at my birth. We were launched, he said. The rest was up to us. Eckart spent too many hours on a window frame in what would become the tenant's apartment while I chiseled mortar from rosy brick in the kitchen. We were in dreamland while the electricians festooned the ceilings with BX cable and then left, slinging their work bags over their shoulders. We didn't know that contracts didn't include closing ceilings and refitting moldings.

In early September, just weeks before she would die of a stroke, proud of our purchase, we led my ninety-three-year-old Viennese Grandma Tess around the torn up garden apartment. She leaned against me, breathing heavily, and looked into my face with cloudy blue eyes, with disbelief. Her hand, as always, in mine.

"*Meine susse, meine susse, was machst du.*" To bring a baby here?"

We assured her it would be fixed, all would be fine in just a few months, in time for the baby. We made her listen to our plans as she sighed and smoothed her skirt with her palms as she always did when she worried. Her next visit would be to hold her great-grandchild. I promised her that. Within the month, she died of a stroke, and at her funeral I kept away from her coffin, determined not ever to remember the mask replacing her face, determined to protect my baby from the loss of this woman who had shown me what unconditional love could feel like.

Grandma Tess, retired with my Grandpa Herman to Hollywood, had sent packages of tartan skirts and matching tams for me when I was four. She created them from photographs sent to their Hollywood bungalow. The clothes fit perfectly; tucked in, amidst the soft plaid material were ceramic heart-shaped boxes, fired in her kiln in the backyard, filled with delicious butter cookies, also shaped into hearts. This grandma I have yet to meet will show me what adoration feels like, her hands stroking mine will remain indelible. When she has moved back to Manhattan following Herman's death, she will declare in many of our visits, in her Viennese accent, "Anything my eyes can see, my hands can make." And hug me to her powdery talcum scent.

I'd been an editor at *Cavalier,* a men's hunting and fishing magazine aspiring to reinvent itself, until the end of my seventh month, rejected the editor-in-chief's offer to continue part-time, and instead, became general contractor for our undercapitalized renovation. Having decided to leave the wider world, I was as determined to be a full-time Madonna as I was to deliver without drugs. In between chores and errands, I practiced my breathing and visualized success with natural childbirth, while workmen came and went, mostly undoing one another's handiwork. Unfazed, I tiptoed around and through the debris, the coiled cables lying across the dust-smeared parquet floor, still in dreamland.

As the date grew near, our part of the house was almost uninhabitable, a tumbled-down construction site with more details of my childhood than I could see then.. If color could be a *madeleine,* the gloomy ochre stairwell was my ticket back to the brownstone apartments of my Village childhood, to the shadows that came with the high ceilings, to my parents' ill-fitting alliance.

The December evening we drove to the Manhattan hospital was strangely balmy, a warm wind stirring the branches on our block, just as the folklore had predicted. Our race across the Brooklyn Bridge was followed by sixteen hours of labor in which our son's forehead was imprinted with the ring of my cervix. Determined to be awake for what was now an emergency Cesarean kept me trapped in contractions, as the spinal was attempted again and again. Finally, the doctor who'd been too late in getting across town barked, "Put her out!"

Twelve hours later, back in my bed, I realized if I lay perfectly still, I could avoid the pull of many needles. From anesthesia and from the long time in recovery, my tongue stuck to the roof of my mouth. The call buzzer was out of reach. My private room was too private. It was 1969 and despite the Lamaze craze, they didn't bring my son to me for nearly two days. Suspended between waves of nausea and dizziness, I had to be reminded that we had our healthy baby boy.

I was listening for my mother's step. She was expected any minute and her footstep was always recognizable. Eckart said she walked like a general, except when she was depressed. I imagined her British brogues striking the linoleum outside my door. I couldn't imagine she wouldn't come near my bed. Unable to lift my head, I send my wordless message... *touch my hair, take my hand...* when they'd opened me to get the baby, they'd also opened that deep longing for her.

"You can't imagine what I went through when she was born! They cut me up, tubes running in and out of me!" She cried out to my college roommate, Sybil, who'd driven her to the hospital. She stayed clear of my bed and after a few minutes announced she was ready to go, to be delivered back to her apartment. Years later, Sybil said she'd nearly opened the car door to throw Bea out onto Columbus Avenue as she carried on about her own Caesarean all the way home to 72nd

Street. I'd sometimes thought of her as "Bea" after graduating, after I'd left home. My father never referred to her as "your Mother" once he'd also left. Years later, I will remember her letters to me, a little girl at camp, signed "Bea"—in parenthesis, "Mother."

It would be another twenty-four hours before I met our son. The bed was still so festooned with tubing that I wondered how they would give him to me without one of us getting entangled in plastic lines, which made me feel helpless, instead of the powerful *deliverer* I'd intended to be.

"Here's your Tiger Man!" The Jamaican nurse beamed, nearly singing, as she settled Nicholas into the crook of my arm.

"We love him in de nursery... dis little man cries only for good reason!" And with that, she was gone.

I knew he couldn't focus, but I stared into his eyes anyway. He yawned and wriggled comfortably. Surprised by what seven pounds felt like, I lifted him to my shoulder. My son's breath was perfectly even on my bare skin. His head rested in the hollow, the nape of my neck. The spot I'd not allowed to be touched since Bea's nails had dug in there. Forty-eight hours after that soft wind, snow had begun to fall and was sticking to the window sill. I didn't know that the center of my life had shifted and would never be the same.

Eckart carried Nicholas up the stone stoop, while I held onto the crumbling banister. The cut in my abdomen was tight, every step a test. I could hear the strains of a Bach welcome, coming from the second floor. How had he arranged the music for our arrival? He'd tuned to QXR before he left for the hospital and hoped for the best, had hoped the music would take the edge off the shock that awaited me as we reached the disheveled bedroom floor, where we would camp out until its kitchen was relocated. His frame of reference was his wartime childhood in Germany and growing up in years of reconstruction. Gaping walls and plaster dust meant nothing to him. I held my sleeping infant above the throbbing scar and made my way through the debris to the tiny hall bedroom Eckart promised would be a nursery when I returned. These are the days when a Caesarean could keep a woman in the hospital for ten days.

"You promised! You said it was finished . . . "

"I thought the music would take the edge off . . . ," he grinned like a teenager.

The pock-marked walls were hastily spackled and the floors still encrusted with years of old paint, revealed by the linoleum we'd peeled back before I went into labor. I saw my Grandma's puzzled face and her watery eyes, clouded by cataracts. Where, she was asking, is the baby nurse to help you? (She'd long ago realized that Bea could not be called upon.) Even a part-time helper had never been considered, for until the construction was completed, there was nothing and everything to clean up.

Sunlight and Bach reached the middle of the room. The shutters would eventually be painted. The rumpled bed was, after all, ours. We put our son in the middle of the quilts. I smiled at my husband, determined to keep my baby safe, especially now, from my murderous disappointment in his father.

Eckart spent the weekend with us, but on Monday was off to Manhattan. I'd watched him dress for the office with a stab of envy and felt a heave of panic as I heard the front door close downstairs. Still in my robe, bent slightly forward to avoid pulling the stitches, I held Nicholas against my shoulder and ventured into the old tenant's kitchen to heat water for tea. There was fine dust everywhere and a draft coming through the ancient ill-fitting windows. The backyard was in its winter shroud, the sky low with clouds. I was too weak from the surgery to plan anything other than staying indoors. The whole day was before me.

The fear of being alone in this place with my newborn dissolved as soon as I felt him relax into another nap, this time on my shoulder. His tiny body comforted me as much as I was supposed to comfort him. I can do this, I told myself as the kettle hissed and, with one free hand, I stretched for a mug. Just as I turned from the stove, a jagged chunk of the plaster ceiling crashed down into the frying pan with its remnants of scrambled egg. Clouds of dust rose from the burners. The sound of plaster on metal vibrated in the tiny space. My baby cried out, as I lurched from the doorway, spilling tea down the front of my robe. I set the mug down on a table cluttered with tools. Nicholas was howling, as I settled into Grandma Tess's worn velvet wing chair to nurse him, to calm both of us. My fingers traced the fontanel on the top of his downy head, the space in his skull that would not be fully closed for months. As if she'd slipped into the room, I heard my mother say, after one of the electroshock treatments at the sanatorium, "... the top of a baby's head ... so friendly." As my breathing matched his, I stopped trembling. I didn't know then that adrenaline will run its course, like an hourglass. And I also didn't know how his birth had brought Bea into more rooms than I could imagine and had opened boxes long closed when I'd kept her at bay.

When he was asleep, I put him on our sunlit bed and lay beside him, listening for his sighs. I scanned the ceiling in this front room for more signs of collapse. I didn't know enough about old plaster. Eckart would have to figure it out after having the supper I hated cooking in the bombed-out kitchen. *Trapped* was the feeling I had to cancel as well as the sense I'd had when labor had started—that Eckart wasn't there for me—had never, in our years together, been undivided. Because that was unbearable to examine, the mess became the distraction from the foreboding worry that he'd fallen in love with someone else. Demolition would become the perfect metaphor for us. I couldn't admit how abandoned, how broken I felt and, instead, focused on the miseries of fixing up a hundred-and-fifty-year-old brownstone with no capital—instead of looking at the terrifying prospect of life as a single mother, bound to be as lost and crazy as my mother was. When I am stripped down to my most fearful, needy self, "Mother" replaces "Bea."

Her first visit had been held off as long as possible, but after a few weeks I stopped making excuses because I could risk it—now that she was in depression again. Her performance at the hospital was still vivid, but my longing for her that day had been submerged. Her depressions still canceled expectation like when I was a child and had exchanged disappointment for fear—the bargain I couldn't know I'd made as I navigated whatever came next. In the corner of Nicholas's tiny room, she took her place in the rocker, waiting for him to be placed in the crook of her arm, as if for a still life in one of her paintings. Nicholas (not yet "Nico") watched her intently, relaxed in his flannel blanket and his now familiar corner. He didn't seem to notice how *unheld* he was. Yearning for her to come closer to me at the hospital merged in that moment with her unsure hold on my baby, her arm stiff. But suddenly she murmured, "The top, the top of a baby's head ... so friendly." as she had that day at the Westchester sanatorium, after another electroshock treatment. Was she referring to something she'd known for a long time? Not a new idea, with this new baby? She handed him back to me and without another word, left the room.

After she'd departed for Manhattan, I wondered, once again, if there'd been a time when we'd been connected, when some instinct to protect me had been in play. It was unfair, to have assumed she could drop him. That wave of muscle memory could have been my own invention. No one could prove that thirty years ago she wasn't capable with me. My instinct had been to snatch him from her, but instead I planted myself in the doorway, allowing her the moment with her grandson, giving her the same benefit of the doubt I'd been able to give her when I was four and hadn't yet started measuring what she could give—against what I wished for.

On that first visit with her new grandchild, my rage and longing entangled and continued to frame this tableau of my mother and my child. When she is tender with him I will have a tantalizing waft of memory and wonder if she was gentle with me? But when she rattles on, ignoring him, I'll feel murderous. No one had ever reported that Bea had been cruel to me as an infant. In fact, my father said she was proud of me (as an infant? a toddler?), but as I answered Nico's cries, I sensed she'd not held me fast. Unsteady she'd been, unsteady would be my inheritance, if I wasn't vigilant. I slipped too easily into the old film, obsessed with foreboding and dread that our small unit of three would also break apart. As a little girl I always imagined the worst, instead of leaving it to chance, to surprise, which I'd learned could be dangerous. This habit (and emotions are habitual) will not serve me well nor will it prevent anything, as it's only the illusion of control.

I would not accept a baby nurse or even a neighborhood woman to help—the mother substitute who might have derailed the collision course I was on. Alone in a broken house, in slower recovery from surgery than a regular birth, I was inescapably reunited with Bea. Instead of congratulating myself on *not* being her, becoming a mother had allowed her back in. As I rocked or watched Nico sigh in sleep, I'd hear her beautiful voice, before Thorazine turned it to a crackling staccato, singing to me at bedtime and I'd murmur "Mom" before I could catch myself... moments with the lost Mother I'd seen in snapshots pasted onto deckle edged black paper, Bea bending over my carriage, her hair gleaming in the sunlight, her smile not exactly confident but winsome, as it would have been called in 1938, her voice soft and sure as she hummed "da de dum da de dum...ah ah baby...," which she still sang when I was four, before becoming the unpredictable, dangerous Mother I had to banish as soon as I knew I was pregnant.

No matter how many times my college friend Gail had said, "You're not your mother," I was secretly terrified of becoming as crazy as she was. The days and nights merged, as all the books said they would, and I was often benumbed or in high worrisome gear unless Nico was in my arms, on my breast, draped across my shoulder—when my old instinct with kittens and puppies prevailed, telling him he was safe. We were safe.

There was some relief to see that Eckart was also thrown back: to the gardens of Plattenburg; imagining a father killed before he could remember him but still imagined from photos; the servants serving tea in the garden and in those photos, which survived the moves and the bombs, his tall, regal mother, Karin, facing the camera, proud of order she made for her small boys in the midst of chaos. Even years later, she did not refer to what they'd endured, only to her triumphs.

I held back confessing to my friends that Nico was as captivating as one of my childhood puppies, that his giddy smiles, waving arms and legs reminded me of the yips and twirls of welcome I'd known from Cokey and Penny and Buffy. And that my fear was like the fear I'd had for my animals—how to keep my baby safe as he teetered on the balls of his feet and walked. I was flying without a net and describing every detail to my worn-out husband when Eckart turned the key in the door after working all day at a job he despised, although we reminded each other, regularly, that we had a Prince, a baby boy whose first days were steady even if we weren't. Mysteriously, I was giving my son what he needed (he was, as the books say, thriving) even as I cataloged my mother's early crimes. I didn't dare invite her often or give the smallest signal I could still be there for her. The baby was my protection. There couldn't be any more midnight rides to Pinewood; she'd have to see I was otherwise occupied, even though I couldn't know that becoming a mother had reunited us.

Despite my fervent, secret wish that my Dad would change his plans for moving to Mexico, he was sticking to his schedule. He'd planned since Nico's birth, in December, to leave in the spring and now it was May. My father and stepmother Clarice were headed for early retirement. His carefree days were coming to him. He'd often boasted of being kicked out of high school for flunking algebra, but then working at a commercial art studio, at seventeen, until his parents gave him one year at the revered National Academy of Art on Fifth Avenue, where he studied with the masters before becoming an illustrator, a commercial artist—a twenty-four-year-old man with a wife and baby during the Great Depression.

Ted and Clarice came to Brooklyn to say good-bye. They walked up our stoop with high color in their cheeks. Done with New York, they were getting out, leaving the city and my mother behind. Despite his declarations of grandfatherly adoration, my father was moving far away at a time when away meant *away.* Tickets and phone calls were costly, but he made a sketch of the little *casita* waiting for us, in the perfect patio they'd found in San Miguel de Allende, and promised invitations. He could still sell me the Brooklyn Bridge. I'd expected a longer visit, but instead they stood for a few minutes in the unpainted living room, neither one asking to hold Nico, who even at seven months was particularly watchful, who knew something was up. Then lickety-split, back down the stoop they went. The station wagon was crammed with every utensil and vase that Clarice couldn't part with; even her worn aluminum frying pan lay on top of mixing bowls. (Amazingly, this same pan will reappear fifteen years later when they return, not to New York but to North Carolina.) My stepmother will cart unworthy objects, as well as heirlooms, back and forth across the border.

Holding Nico with one arm, I stood at the curb and raised the other to wave as the station wagon moved towards the corner. My vision was blurred, my tongue thick. I could barely see the car heading south for the Battery Tunnel. I carried my baby back up the stoop, into the house. Why was my face sleek with sweat, my ears ringing? I reminded myself… they'd hardly been around, had seldom come to visit. As I closed the front door, I murmured, "Nico has a Dad. I have a husband. We are a family."

That night I had the same dream from my college days when I'd been afraid my father would leave Bea with me forever. She and I would sit at opposite ends of a long table, a kind of Thanksgiving table, but one which is missing the platters and guests. There is no conversation in this dream, none of her words that can cut me. I'm holding onto the edge of the table as the room begins to spin.

4

"Here comes the train!" I held the spoon at an angle, the applesauce poised to slip into Nico's open mouth. It was mid-morning. During his early nap I'd given up breakfast for a shampoo. My days were his. I'd leap from the bathtub or race upstairs when piercing cries announced his nap was over. No one had asked me to be his handmaiden. I'd volunteered from the beginning. *Let me get this right,* I implored the invisible taskmaster who accompanied my every move. In the absence of a wise, or not so wise, elder or a friend, I was making it up: doing my mother job as improvisation... confident and worried, confident and opinionated. Beset with self-doubt, swinging between two poles in a single hour, while the film of ambulance rides, with my mother in a straitjacket, sometimes flashed without warning—midnight rides that had happened years before and lay waiting to ensnare me—as I had become a Mom.

Nico was now over a year old. He gazed at me as he mouthed the fruit, delighted with the taste, with the spring breeze, with my smile although my hands shook uncontrollably as the early morning lightheadedness took over. adrenaline surged, leaving me breathless until I gulped down the orange juice, which I learned stopped the shaking. I'd never liked breakfast, had always been an eleven o'clocker (as the Brits say), unable to eat before mid-morning. We were finally using the new kitchen on the parlor floor. The long windows gave a leafy view of the garden, with its Rose of Sharon tree set far back near the fence. These trees were in every neighborhood, a favorite of the Victorians who had made Brooklyn.

Dr. Sandler, the psychiatrist I was seeing for postpartum depression, listened raptly to my description of the latest high chair event of shaking hands and dizziness, alone with my baby.

"Obviously, you don't want to feed your child. You have resentment against him. We must work on this." He intoned, checking his watch, his face as mask-like as ever—the perfect patriarchal Freudian in an era still enshrining the sage. He'd gotten it half-right, the resentment part, but not against Nicholas. Not being touched by his father wasn't something I could say out loud, nor could I bring up the images which suddenly brought Bea into the room—tangles and knots which might, if held to the light, reveal how tight they were.

My time was up. I moved unsteadily towards the door. His office was in the Village, on 11th Street between 5th and 6th. I had come from Brooklyn on the subway. Although the sitter was waiting, I was tempted to wander down 10th Street to see if the doorman at our old building was still alive. I hadn't had breakfast again and my hands were shaking right there in Dr. Sandler's lobby. The aloof Freudian will wait a few more months before declaring that I have a *schicksal neurose* (Freud's term for a fate neurosis). He says I believe I am fated to live my mother's life and can't have anything more than she had. I can't tell you why we never explored his observation, which might have changed this story. As a Freudian, he was probably waiting for it to come from me, the frozen me who couldn't have gone into that forest without the gentle guidance he was incapable of. It will be another year before I will be diagnosed with hypoglycemia, whose symptoms the good Freudian M.D had ignored. In 1971 low blood sugar was not the rage, nor was its connection to postpartum depression widely recognized.

Brownstoners in Brooklyn, in the 1970s, were known for marriages broken before houses were fixed. I'd married a foreigner whose footings in New York were still unproven and had given up my job just before my due date. How could we be tearing up a place that needed tons of money, with hardly enough to cover the costs of basic rewiring? Until walls were opened, I didn't know I wasn't a candidate for this protracted, pinch-penny renovation—and not with a man whose moods were harder and harder to read.

I moved through the day like a purposeful sleepwalker, not seeing how this construction site was a constant reminder of the chaos my mother had created in our apartments. *Not seeing* was my refuge, the protection for our little family. An early Rorschach test had informed my parents when I was in kindergarten, "Linda has difficulty seeing the whole picture." Like so many of you, if I didn't have this deficit, I'd be telling another story.

"Happy!" Nico declared loudly and clearly, for the first time, splashing in his bath, sending water to the edge of the tub. Grinning back at him, I dropped his favorite boat into the water. My early evening fatigue lifted instantly. I was ready for the nightly game that came with drying him off in a big towel, the few minutes of tag that ended in getting him into pajamas. Zooming his Tonka truck across the floor, he shouted out my cousin's names "Anne!" "Guy!" as if he were remembering the afternoon at their house days before. He pushed me sideways on the couch, shouting, "Gotcha!" We made the game up together and it went on for months, never ceasing to delight and embolden him. I was puzzled when Eckart said if only his mother had allowed such games, he might have trusted her more, might not have missed his father so much. This was mixed up and fragmented. Eckart saw symbolism whereas I saw playfulness when I let my toddler push me down. In our Berlin days, when we'd talked for hours, Eckart had said I was nothing like his mother. It was intended as a compliment and came at that early time, when like so many couples, we made a bridge over the bodies of our unsuspecting parents—uniting us even more as we recounted their crimes. How did the children of *perfect* parents ever find their mates? Whatever could they talk about?

"Ma! Come up, the baby's got fever." Our shared brick wall brought Joe and Vera's family into my living room. I wanted to cry out to the ladies in their flowered house dresses, "Come up to me!" as I watched my Italian neighbors moving in battalions to church, to christenings, to wakes, to the cousins in Bay Ridge, to paint their sister's apartment, to interfere, to annoy, to care for one another. Tessie was our next door neighbor. Not my Grandma Tess but an Italian grandmother born in Bari, the heel of Italy's boot. At the trash cans and over our garden gates, she regaled me with tales of her past including a story I'd hear more than once.

"I'll never forget... we all knew Papa had died when Mama got out of the cab, right here in front... we all knew he was dead. She would never have left the hospital if he was breathing. She'd been there for weeks, sleeping on the cot."

I didn't know then how this web of family slammed me with longing, although I was doing my mother job without instruction, but with some reliable instinct. My baby was as sunny a little boy as I'd been told I was as an infant. But the closeness with Eckart, during the pregnancy, was gone. Now he only had eyes for his son; the tenderness he felt for our adorable child was hard to watch. When we admired Nico asleep in his crib, Eckart's arm wasn't around me. His eyes didn't meet mine as our child slept. I was tempted to ask why he was absent, preoccupied, but apprehension was better than actually knowing something. His remoteness had been part of his description from the beginning. It had even been an inducement, as if getting his attention was the prize. Unable to explain his mood swings, he remained a mystery to me. The birth of our son had not solved any of his career issues. It hadn't made his market research work in advertising any more palatable. It seemed he had his own troubles and was compelled to keep them to himself.

With the baby in my belly, everything had seemed possible. Hormones had replaced doubt. Now, the exposed rafters and pock marked walls cast their own spell. From early morning, when the shutters let in the first light, until late in the evening when I finally gave up the watch, I was invaded by low-level panic, like a low-grade fever. Eckart's tenderness during the pregnancy now seemed like a mirage, tantalizing, unreliable. If we made love, he was so distant afterwards that I might have imagined it. And never missing a moment for self-doubt, for taking the blame, I assumed it was my fault. My breasts were too big (I was still nursing), my stomach not flat enough?

This unfamiliar neighborhood was my Siberia. Had I not been seized by panic attacks, I would have been charmed by the man leading his horse down our street, parking his wagon while women sent their children racing with money for the vegetables. Tessie hosed down her walkway each morning, patiently routing out a stray leaf. When I heard the squeak of the wash lines in the backyard … there would be no rain. Flags of boxer shorts, house dresses, and girdles swung in the breeze. There wasn't a bookstore within walking distance, but even if there had been I couldn't have found comfort in my old self. My reading and writing self had vanished along with the person who'd worn L'Air Du Temps. Ever since my son's birth, I'd been sickened by the scent I'd loved for years. I was afraid to admit, even to Eckart, how anxious I felt when I was *not* taking care of Nico. The hours of feeding, the repetitive tasks anchored me. So this was growing a child.

When he napped, I couldn't make good use of the time. Couldn't write or read, couldn't allow myself to be transported. Instead I went deeper into worry that was really a postpartum depression but that I described as nervousness. Along with ignorance of blood-sugar issues, postpartum depression was another mystery yet to be unlocked by the medicine men. The *shame* of the depression, which no one talked about, which I was unable to reveal to anyone but Eckart, was nearly as bad as the depression itself. So what! So you have these weird feelings of doom and guilt. Pull yourself together and be grateful that your baby is perfect—I told myself ten times a day.

5

Seventeen-month-old Nico was greeting the pigeons and waving his hands to music only he could hear on that gorgeous June morning. I'd never taken his stroller on a bus or even more than a few blocks from home, but admiring smiles from middle-aged Italian women in house dresses, hosing down their patch of sidewalk, told me I could do this–despite the postpartum depression that had hung on too long to be called *post* and that had taken every scrap of my fragile confidence as a new mother.

At dawn I'd awakened without the dread of the past months and decided to risk it, to run an errand, like a Regular Mom. I was off to Abraham & Strauss, Brooklyn's oldest department store for a Father's Day gift to send to my Dad, in Mexico, and one for Eckart, from his baby boy. When the bus swerved to the curb, I was helped aboard by one of the retired longshoremen from the social club on our corner.

"Taking the baby downtown?" He smiled as he lifted the carriage.

"A&S. Father's Day is coming." I smiled back, holding Nico tightly in my arms.

"Careful little mother. Take care of the boy," as he headed down the aisle.

The bus lurched to a stop. With Nico on my hip, I carried the stroller like a bangle, on my wrist. Our first bus ride together was, as Eckart would say whenever he found a parking space in Manhattan, already a success: the self-consciousness, the shame of the postpartum nowhere in sight.

I pushed the stroller between the counters in the men's haberdashery, searching for the perfect ascot for a retired advertising man recreating his life, as the artist he'd been before I was born. Instead of a tie, I wanted a rich paisley silk ascot. A sudden slam of June heat had caught the store management off-guard: there was no air conditioning, the air was heavy.

As I leaned over the glass counter my face was struck with shimmering heat from the bulbs. Grabbing the edge of the glass, cold sweat pouring down my back, pulling the stroller to my hip, I slid to the marble floor, engulfed in blackness. It happened in slow motion, the way people describe car crashes. In total darkness, I could still hear my baby shrieking, "Mama! To keep from losing consciousness I attached to his voice. Had he climbed out of the stroller, was he lost in the crowd? Was I blind? It was only seconds lying in darkness before I felt arms under me. As I was lifted onto a wheelchair there was bright light, faces peering into mine. Nico's color was as high as I'd seen it, his cheeks flaming, bangs plastered against his forehead. Still strapped into his stroller, shrieking and waving his arms, he reached for me. I cried out, "Give him to me!" The instant he settled against my chest, we both stopped trembling. I stopped sobbing.

I didn't take my eyes off my son to see who was pushing the wheelchair. An employee elevator took us to First Aid on the tenth floor. The nurse settled him onto the narrow cot with me and handed him the plastic bears dangling from the stroller. His hair was still wet against his forehead, but with my hand on his back he was quiet and calm, the bears snug in his lap. We were both given orange juice.

"We've called your husband's office and left a message." Her Brooklyn accent was reassuring, even motherly, like the women on our block who didn't know I wanted them to adopt me ever since the birth of my beautiful boy.

Surely, it wouldn't be long before Eckart would come for us. I breathed deeply, mimicking the Lamaze lessons that had not carried me through the delivery but might carry me through this. My tongue was thick, and my eyes still weren't working right. Nico was busy with his bears, and before long the nurse handed me the phone.

"Please ... come get us," I said in a whisper, as if a whisper would bring him. "The nurse says your blood pressure is fine. You're okay."

"I'm scared, really scared. It was out of the blue. I couldn't see! I could hear but couldn't see! Please come for us." I was sobbing. I'd wait all day for him in that pale green cubicle.

"Take a cab! For God's sake, just take a cab," his voice in that chilly register I'd heard, but denied, for months. The nurse helped me to my feet, waited with Nico while I used the restroom, and then told me it was company policy to be escorted to the street in a wheelchair. I was too shaky to protest, to admit it was mortifying to retrace our steps, again in the wheelchair. Instead of giving myself a break, humiliation and shame would haunt me—for leaving my shrieking baby boy as everything went dark. I won't know for years that being in public was crowded with images of my manic depressive mother acting up, wild as wind, even when she's nowhere in sight, that one nightmare was inexorably linked to others—the tangle of us.

Before we set out for the main floor, I called our friends Henry and Sheila, who lived just blocks away. We'd kept in touch since our days as counselors at a summer camp in Quebec. When Henry married Sheila, who'd become a doctor, they'd come to West Berlin, for Henry to finish research for his dissertation. My German Information Press junket long completed, I was living on Niebuhrstrasse with Eckart. Taking a cab to Sheila and her children would be better than being home alone with Nico in our brownstone, still ramshackle, still not welcoming.

By six in the evening Sheila said my color was normal, my eyes bright. Although I told her I could hear but couldn't see when I fell, she didn't connect my description with a *vasovagal syncope* or *vagus nerve* blackout, in which you don't lose consciousness, as in fainting, but cannot see for several seconds. Hypoglycemia is one of its triggers. I didn't mention I'd skipped breakfast in my hurry to get going on what was meant to be a kind of celebration.

Even though we were five years from living in Germany, as Eckart came through their doorway, I was still programmed to see him as my guide. And more importantly, the man who'd created a shield between me and my manic depressive mother when we'd returned to New York. He greeted our friends warmly and tossed his son into the air, then pulled me against his jacket as if to say, "We're a family. I'm here now" his stony self nowhere in sight.

Later that night, as we got into bed, he said firmly, "Now don't make a big deal of this!" then turned his back and retreated into sleep. Instead of leaning into him, instead of being held, I went to Nico's crib and, in darkness, listened to his breathing. And spent the rest of the night beside my son's crib, not touching the man who'd become more and more mysteriously distant—the silhouette of a husband.

I won't know for years that he is as imprisoned as I am in this marriage. In that darkness I also didn't know how much rage was fueled by his refusal to come for us and that rage was too dangerous and had to be replaced with fear. Fear was acceptable. *Fury* was for crazy women like my mother, whose husbands leave, as my father did. With fear in place, and fury safely off-stage, phobia would be the next stop—for a train that had left the station.

6

With pleasure and excitement, we accepted an invitation to my brother-in-law's wedding in England. It was Nico's second summer. We were transported out of the falling-to-pieces house to an Inn, with swans paddling in a stream that wound through rolling lawns. This was the England of my college fantasies, where Bloomsbury's genteel literati had repaired to the country. If I could step into the drawing rooms of Edwardian England, could I leave this fearful, phobic self behind like the skin snakes leave in the underbrush?

Our adorable boy scandalized the guests by crowing throughout the ceremony, confirming their Anglo belief that American children were doomed just by being in the hands of parents who had no breeding. Although I was subdued at the reception, I was able to chat with the guests, feel ever so slightly like my old self, notice the dense green of the new grass, and laugh with others as Eckart described his childhood escapade—the swans he tormented as he swung them over his head, ignoring his mother's warning that swans could take off the hand of a little boy. And how he pulled the tablecloth off the tea table set in the garden, sending cups flying and suffering the whacks his mother administered to his backside.

When Eckart returned to work in New York, we'd planned for me and Nico to spend a few days with my glamorous cousins in their London apartment overlooking Cavendish Square. Daring to visit

Bill and Florence seemed a signal that the crazies were gone, that the A&S blackout—which I didn't describe, even to myself, as a sign of Eckart's abandonment—was safely in the past, not in that storage unit where we park our fears and rage.

When Nico and I awoke to the clip clop of horse's hooves and a faint drum beat, we ran to the window to see the Queen's cavalry guard just below us. With tall fur hats and red jackets, they waited just a few yards from my little boy shrieking and waving, his cheeks flaming, his eyes shining. The memory would be mine. At twenty months, my son was still in the present tense.

Florence urged me to explore Harrods when Nico napped. Having raised three daughters, she reassured me that she knew a thing or two about toddlers. She didn't know her offer was more like a dare. I checked and rechecked my purse for my passport, money, my passport, money. I even wrote down the address of the building I was about to leave. As I started across the street, a wave of nausea forced me back onto the curb. My palms were wet. Suddenly the light was too bright in the gray sky. I looked down, pretending to check my shoes, then straightened up and moved ahead, hoping it was a kind of stage fright, not a full-blown panic attack. My purposeful stride was calming, one two three one two three. Instead of moving like others headed purposefully to their destinations, I wondered if I was as split-off and distracted as Mrs. Dalloway? Did I need to invoke the legendary Virginia Woolf to frame yet another attack? Couldn't I just leave my boy asleep in a safe place and have a few hours of pleasure?

When I spotted a children's bookstore in the middle of the block and crossed the threshold, my breathing slowed as I was able to browse the shelves; to focus on the drawings and typefaces of the exquisite books printed in Holland. I chose a picture book about the moon leading a family home. The way it had led me home as a little girl on those late night car trips with my parents, when my mother calmed by a day in the country and my father at the helm, steered us safely back to 10th Street. Just as Nico will soon whisper, "The moon is following us" when Eckart will drive the three of us home to Second Place.

Despite the recent A&S nightmare, I dared myself to enter Harrods, where I was surprised to be able to move easily between the crowded counters of tartan, cashmere, boar head bristle hair brushes, oatmeal soap and shortbread biscuits. England was, after all, reassuring. I didn't have another black out episode of instant terrifying darkness. When I retraced my steps to my cousin's apartment, Mrs. Woolf was at my side, as if we'd been to tea. Even though she'd succumbed, unable to be comforted, I could and would be. These spells would be just that, *spells*.

Eckart welcomed us back at JFK with a bear hug, taking both of us in his arms at once. Home again, home again jiggity-jig, until he blurted out that the whole Israeli team at the Munich Olympics had been killed that day. His feelings about his Jewish wife and son must have been buried in the shocking news, which I noted, but didn't bring up. Once more, not knowing was safer. I'd felt his ambivalence in West Berlin, knew in some murky, convoluted way he blamed the Jews, not Hitler, for his father's death, and knew that he, unlike so many "good" young Germans, had not visited the camps. And yet I'd buried the information and stayed with him, my need for protection overwhelming information. Thousands of miles away, my mother was still framing my story.

Our neighbor's pear tree was in bloom, spreading its creamy blossoms across our shared backyard fence. I could go about my business, as Dr. Sandler had instructed, the business of being content with my beautiful child and my handsome, mysterious husband.

7

"Don't shout at a boy who is nice! Don't shout at a boy who is happy!" Nico was giving it back to his father, who had reprimanded him in a rare moment of assertion. Our shared policy was to negotiate with our son. When he is grown and looking for clues for what wasn't right in his childhood, he'll tell us we were too soft and didn't prepare him for a world which might not find him as perfect as we did.

Nico's third birthday was coming up. By now, the trip to England which felt like a return to normal life had been followed with episodes of dizziness and "panic attacks" which weren't called that in 1973. Ever since the incident at A&S when Nico was seventeen months old, shame had become my constant companion. We're thirty years away from wearing phobias like a badge. And crazy mothers could only reveal themselves if you hadn't been warned by your Dad to hide your mother's sickness from any serious swain. Gay husbands and wives were still in the underground unless you were part of a woman's group who were, among other things, urging each other to place mirrors in front of their vaginas so that "down there" would no longer be mysterious.

I was missing the women's movement because it wasn't a tutorial and besides, getting to a meeting was too terrifying. Having one in my own living room was equally impossible. Where had I disappeared to?

When will I return? When will it be safe to be outside again? These were the questions, as steady as rain, as I cared for my son, made meals and avoided places where panic escalated—where my vision went a little nuts and my breathing mimicked a heart attack.

After months of consulting doctors, who had no idea what had befallen me, there was finally a diagnosis of hypoglycemia, still rare in the early Seventies. Instead of being reassured by a physical cause for my shakiness and lightheadedness, which came close to losing consciousness, the discovery confirmed my secret belief that I'd always been as damaged as my mother, that no man I wanted would want to marry me—until in West Berlin, Eckart had said emphatically, "Not important! Everyone has someone crazy in the family."

Omnipresent cheese and nut packets, at the ready for a drop in blood sugar, didn't reassure me. None of my doctors made the connection between hypoglycemia, depression and *agoraphobia,* which was mostly mispronounced, derived from the Greek *agora* or market place and *phobi*a, meaning irrational fear. Paradoxically, the official description cites fear of open spaces as well as fear of crowds and narrow spaces. The seeds of the disorder could be multiple, but depression would always be at the top of the list, as well as trauma triggering the disorder—which had been blacking out in Brooklyn's most famous department store and my husband's response. I will never know what might not have happened if Eckart had come for us that day, taken us in his arms, taken us home.

It will be years before agoraphobia will be described as a disorder that requires treatment and will not go stealthily away as it had come.

46

Every agoraphobic has unconsciously designated where he can or cannot go, under which circumstances, and with whom. Much like a functional alcoholic, some of us can leave the house with a safe person and can move in a small grid—to the playground, a school conference, a neighborhood restaurant—but only with that designated driver, the enabler who will ideally act as if this is no big deal, as my neighbor Evie did again and again.

The art and not the science now, so many years later, tells me that I was programmed for this particular fall, even if one of the components had been out of the equation. The cheese and nuts I carried weren't a match for my conviction that I was, after all, my mother's daughter; fated to live her story—not my own.

The shame of my public disgrace in Abraham & Straus triggered avoidance—which is guaranteed to keep one frozen. In warm weather, the unusual front and back gardens of our block made it easy. Without going past the front garden gate, I could take care of Nico in his small world of tricycles and Big Wheels, too ashamed to join the other women chatting over the wrought iron fences. Nico and I were both counting: I was counting the steps to the corner where I needed to buy bread, and he was counting to "twenty" as he watched the cat lap her milk or climbed the stairs to his room. The longshoremen hanging around Frank's deli who'd been jolly to me when I was pregnant, ebullient, must have wondered why I waited at the counter more frozen than quiet, avoiding eye contact with Frank and his wife, Anne, hoping to keep at bay the small talk I could no longer manage. The confident, blooming young woman was nowhere in sight. The symptoms were increasing: ringing in my ears accompanied the dizziness and a thick pressure on my windpipe that came and went without warning.

When I heard of a new doctor in the neighborhood making house calls like the old timers, it was a relief not to ask Eckart to make yet another trip with me. He'd confessed that when he walked the block home from the subway, he dreaded a new detail. Would I be cheerful, when would life be normal again? The home visit with the new neighborhood doctor held out hope. Might I be returned to that other young woman whose hormones were doing their job, who'd come to Carroll Gardens more excited than fearful.

As I opened the glass-paned door to greet the doctor, the young man in the sports jacket and dark shirt was a surprise. He was more collegiate than medical and surely not from the neighborhood. As I led him past the ever present construction debris, I was prepared to tell him that I couldn't have come to his office alone and that it was terrifying to wake in the morning with my heartbeat in my ears. Before I could begin, he had taken my blood pressure, felt my throat for swollen glands, and checked my ears. His movements were nearly athletic, his touch rough.

"Doctor, something's really wrong with me."

"You! You are a perfectly healthy woman who has wasted my time!" He sneered, shut his leather bag and turned to leave in one motion, like a golfer.

That evening I made a special dinner. As Eckart and I faced each other in the candle light, signaling the worst of the day was past, I couldn't tell him the doctor had humiliated me for fear he'd agree with him, would damn me as the doctor had, would let his rage fly at me, sending me back to the moment in the green cubicle—when I'd heard his icy detachment, instead of the promise to come for us. And had no clue that his refusal echoed my father's disappearance and his insistence that I be the one on the jump seat of the ambulances carrying Bea and me into the night.

I didn't need to invent a description of the doctor's visit. Eckart didn't ask for one as he dug into the meal I'd fussed over and kept warm for his usual late arrival. Held fast by phobias which were doing their job of keeping this family together, it didn't occur to me that my entrapment also served his agenda.

Although Bea hadn't been in a mental hospital in years, I didn't trust her to be interested in what had happened to me. Instead I dreamed of her alone, eating alone, sitting on the Madison Avenue bus, all alone with no one else on board. I'm not with her but am watching her in this film. I allowed her to visit me in my dreams because I was limiting her access to our house. Her arrival at Second Place was always too big a deal: her navigations on the subway were recounted like Hillary on Everest instead of admitting that subways frightened her, that she had never gotten over her father dying of a heart attack on a platform. If that had been out in the open, I might have connected my own subway phobia with the guy who'd followed me up the steps and grabbed under my skirt as I had exited at 23rd Street, on the way to Head Start, my first post-college job. I'd have known that my grandfather dying on a subway platform was what she'd passed to me, long before that scary morning on my way to work—just as when I see a mother pulling her small child back from a passing dog, even on a leash, I'm witnessing a planting as deep as any row of corn.

Before my mother-in-law's Christmas visit, I was determined to walk up Clinton Street to the library. I hadn't gone this far from our block since that morning at Abraham & Straus. I had to prove I could do something as normal as walking to the library before Karin arrived. She would be bringing her ever-present microscope. The one I'd felt from our first meeting in Munich years before. I'd always been self-conscious with her, but now I had more than a thing or two to be self- conscious about.

After leaving Nico with Evie, I turned up Second Place to Clinton Street. Under a flat steel-gray sky, I kept my head down, my eyes on the sidewalk. Barely able to keep my balance on the uneven cement, I tightened my scarf and walked more quickly, my eyes downcast... *count the paved squares to the corner... if I make it to the corner I can make four more blocks.*

With the wind at my back, I counted the steps to the end of the wrought iron fence leaving me at the corner of First Place. Three more blocks. I can't meet anyone who knows me... *please let me get there without a fall, without lying flat on the cement.* I reached the wide steps of the library just in time to sit down before I was in blackness, hearing the passing cars just as I'd heard the saleslady at the tie counter. The cold stone could have been the marble floor. The darkness was as terrifying as the first time but there was a weird sense of familiarity, as if I knew it would end and I would see the steps, the sidewalk, just as before, like a stop action film. I was simultaneously afraid and relieved, relieved to be alone on the steps, not on the floor in haberdashery with strangers staring. When my legs could work, I stood and turned back down Clinton Street, too shaken to get the book I'd come for. Home, home free, just let me get there. Let me fill the tub for Nico's bath, let me broil the chops let me sing him to sleep. And let me light the candles and not describe this walk to Eckart, who was now more Nico's father than my husband.

8

Dr. Mallman's office, being located in the Heights, was even more important than his solid reputation as a Freudian analyst. His tentative manner and hushed voice was a relief from the austere, sonorous pronouncements I'd gotten from Dr. Sandler. Sharing a first name with my father, Theodore (both used Ted) was the kind of coincidence that we can notice, ponder, or just leave alone. On our first meeting, as I described the panic that ruled my days, he removed his glasses and leaned forward in his chair as if to say—we're in this together.

I left the office, high on the possibility that this man could help me, could assure me that I wasn't crazy after all—or if I was, he'd bring me back, help me to walk back into my life, albeit not a picture postcard but one in which I moved about, without counting every step, back to the life I'd left when I'd walked back into our house with Eckart that June evening after the A&S nightmare, the trigger for the agoraphobia, which now held me hostage.

In those first weeks, I dared to walk a few blocks, before leaping into a cab. I told a few friends I was getting new help. I also did what was to be expected: I responded to Mallman's acceptance with love, that same devotion I'd felt for my professors.

Everything about him moved me: his cactus collection arranged on the teakwood cube. "I like to make things grow," he said quietly, the way he said everything else; the overly tidy office suggesting a careful person, his attempts to be modish with navy shirts and dark ties, and particularly his warm brown eyes in contrast to thin, often pursed lips. Those thin lips seemed in harmony with the precise arrangements of books, pencils in mugs, and tissues near the patient's chair, but his eyes were the surprise: when he removed his steel rimmed glasses they were dark pools of empathy, which I memorized like other times I'd been seduced; then replayed the sessions so as not to lose a minute of the pleasure. *Pleasure* was back, although L'Air Du Temps behind my ears still didn't smell like it had before Nico's birth.

In the way that analysts like to go deeper into the woods, before finding the path that might lead you out, Mallman listened to my endless tales of woe. Until the day he leaned forward, looked deeply into my eyes and said my phobias were as much my creation as any dinner I'd ever cooked, or book I was trying to write, or the child I was raising.

"I intend," he said softly, "to come between you and your phobias."

If that wasn't enough, he also intended to drive a wedge between me and my parents. This Flatbush intellectual, this paragon of bourgeois virtue was going to take on as many cans of worms as necessary to get me better. I can't know then that analysis doesn't make agoraphobics better.

When I'd been with a man who intrigued me, I'd always found simplest declarations nearly impossible: *tired* or *hungry* was never announced. Better to be a wood nymph needing nothing more than a song to live on, but with Mallman I could announce firmly, "I won't lie on the couch. I want to look at you, to see your eyes. And I want you to talk," declaring my own little war on patriarchal Freudian protocol because it seemed I could. Unlike the frozen sessions with Dr. Sandler, these meetings were full of possibility. Within a few weeks I brought him a dream, the first of many offerings.

"I'm in the basement of a farmhouse in Greece, one I was in years ago with a poet. It's just as it was, white walls, little furniture … except the man isn't Leonard, it's you."

"What am I doing?" He asked in an obliging whisper.

"You're washing me, rinsing off the soap with buckets of water." My cheeks were fiery. He removed his glasses as he did when he was fully listening.

"I'm having this shower and the sun's streaming through the lower window and I've put up my arms to be rinsed all over and it is you, not the poet, who's washing me."

Walking home, I tripped and fell to the sidewalk. When I called to report falling, he interrupted his machine to take my call, making it bearable to wait a whole week to see him again.

He moved ever so carefully across his long-wearing, industrial carpet that it took a while to notice the spring in his step and to guess correctly he was a tennis player. His hands told me he also played the piano, but his choreographed, gentle movement had me asking if he ever threw a chair at his wife. He blushed and was silent.

In the next session he challenged me to go behind my recitation of doubt and fear, "You know, of course, that your troubles make you special. If you can't excel at your work, can't do your profession, then at least, your neurosis will tell the world you're someone to be noticed."

Like many of his fellow Freudians, at that time, he painted in few colors, not a full palette, which would have included my mother and my husband entangled in the mystery of my imprisonment. The job of phobia's wasn't identified by Mallman and wouldn't be clear for several more years. All he said was that they were my creation—not what those boundaries were meant to do.

On Easter Sunday, a small, blond puppy ran up our front stoop and wandered through our open door. It was unseasonably warm for early April. Evie and I'd been chatting in the strong sunlight, as the kids from the block careened in and out of our front garden. The pup raced through to the kitchen. In that instant I knew I couldn't put him back on the street, even if Nico hadn't sped after him, calling, "Mommy, Mommy! You won't put him out, right?"

We bathed the yellow puppy before Eckart came home. I gave up trying to decide how many breeds he was made of, but as the week passed I wasn't prepared to deal with his hysterical personality, not just puppy-hysterical but the hysteria of a young dog that's been lost or thrown out. The small boys did their best to excite him until they had him nipping at their legs and finally, drawing blood.

I kept up my daily calls to Bide-a-Wee (a no-kill shelter) and was rewarded with a spot for him. Instead of feeling firm in my decision, I began the torturous dance of separating from this little dog. The month-long indecision about *puppy puppy,* as he was called (instead of a name that would have made him ours forever), became one of my more quintessential foot-on brake-foot-on-accelerator gambits.

The list of *Lasts* was growing: this dinner was the last time I'd see him mournful, as he waited under the table for scraps, the last time he'd leap around the kitchen until Eckart came home and puppy puppy headed for safety on his cushion and the last time I would allow myself to really look into his eyes. He'd kept his distance from Eckart, so that morning it was up to me to trick him, to snap the lead onto his makeshift collar. Eckart pulled *puppy puppy* out the front door with his hind legs splayed and his head down. The relief I'd expected was nowhere in sight. I didn't know then that rescue was embedded in me, as deeply as any DNA, and that I'd been drawn to Eckart, having been unable to rescue Bea. Nor did I know that repeated rescuing—be it animals or people who cross our path—is often a repeated rescuing of ourselves.

Mallman tried to ease the hideous remorse I felt in the days that followed. He also seized the moment.

"When you gave up the dog, you put yourself in your mother's role... and now you're full of guilt, self-doubt. By becoming the person who abandons, you wanted her to feel what she'd done to you and because you know she'll never feel it, you felt it for her. To make sure she suffers for what she did to you."

Although his analysis remained *his* and not the ah-ha moment I was hoping for, this get-out-of-jail moment led me to see that whatever was holding me fast, was connected to Bea, to the mother who wasn't the mother. What I didn't know then is how Bea's fate had drawn me to my brooding husband—get her attention, get his... fix

56

her, make him laugh… whatever the cost. After all those boyfriends, had I been waiting for Eckart? And how had our tensions and Eckart's distancing, after sex, escaped Mallman's attention no matter how often I described it all?

Freudian therapy was not taking me far enough. I could barely navigate the mile home, could just go into a few shops and carry back supplies that had been delivered for years. But, shamefully, still couldn't risk walking that same mile to the Heights, to cross Atlantic Avenue with my little boy, risk him seeing his Mom in a full blown panic attack splayed out on the sidewalk or even in a black-out, which this time he would remember. Would he hate me for getting bad attention? Would he keep his distance then, as I'd kept mine from Bea? These worries prevented me from seeing I'd already *not* been her in his first years. They were the way I sabotaged any sense of accomplishment—that my son was, despite his mother's craziness, thriving.

As many times as we dissected the mystery he insisted was my creation, Mallman had nothing more to offer, no clues to what the phobia was protecting, nothing to break the spell I lived under every day. I said goodbye to him with as much *élan* as I could muster—like ending an affair.

9

My father surprised us with plane tickets for a visit to San Miguel. Although I couldn't get to the grocery store on Court Street, the trip to see his new house, the patios, and the gardens he'd described seemed possible. I'd missed my charismatic, unreliable father and wanted to be in his walled patio, filled with flowering vines, where I imagined us, finally, talking as we hadn't for years, maybe ever. As I went about my daily routine I felt lighter, imagining the gardens and my father's greeting at the airport. We were, after all, always very good at entrances.

Because it was 1974 and we were in Carroll Gardens, where longshoremen kept our block safe, we were careless about closing our kitchen windows at night. Our cat Tusie didn't roam after dark. She stayed curled behind Nico, sleeping amidst all the stuffed animals who kept him company. She was not only his cat but his nanny, following him around and running to him when he fell. (When he's grown, Tusie will have made Nico into a cat person and not a dog person like his mother.)

That May morning, as first light filtered through the shutter, I heard a cat's screeching, piercing yowl—but couldn't be sure it was our Tusie. In a flash, Eckart's bare heels hit the treads as he flew down the stairs. More yowls, then the higher pitched screams of cats in combat. As I moved towards the landing, his bellow stopped me, "Stay there! Do not come down!" his accent stronger than usual.

Nico is sleeping, I told myself. This detail about my sleeping boy was most important as I sat on the edge of the bed in a pool of sweat. Eckart doesn't want you to see Tusie lying on the kitchen floor, her blood running… your safe person is protecting you after all.

"That son of a bitch tom was after her. Tusie's okay. He won't be back." Eckart called out from the landing, already on his way to the shower. *This his little boy could hear.*

I repeated silently, *Nico is asleep, still asleep, miraculously sleeping* and sat where I was told to stay, on the rumpled sheet until Eckart returned and opened the top shutter, as he always did first thing. He told me not to open the garbage can at our gate, in the sunlight, the same sunlight streaming across our bed. As he stood in front of the mirror, knotting his tie, he declared he'd axed Tessie's orange tom, not a house cat, but her cat just the same. The ax was with other garden tools against the wall instead of where it should have been in the garden shed. He didn't look at me as he spoke, just finished dressing, as intent upon his preparations as any other morning when he escaped Second Place. Had killing the orange cat been impulsive, like stepping on a spider?

A few minutes before, in our kitchen, the person who'd been protection from my insane mother became the insane person who killed Tessie's cat even when ours was already out the window. I was hanging onto the bed while the room swirled, colors collided, and I tried to focus as I had at A&S. But this time I didn't black out. I talked to myself. My job was to be calm, to give Nico breakfast, to get him ready for a play-date with Josh, and to greet Evie without a word that my husband had axed our neighbor's cat to death instead of chasing him out like other times. If I told her I'd be tempted to confess I imagined the orange tabby was a stand-in for me, that Eckart's silences were instead of chopping me up. This exaggeration danced before me even as I knew it was an exaggeration. Sometimes the fantastical carries information.

That evening all he said was he was sick of strays coming through the window, sick of attacks on our cat. If I wanted to turn this into a major event, be my guest, he offered—his jaw clenched, like the night after we'd come home from Henry and Sheila's. I didn't say if you ever do that again I'm gone because we both knew I could hardly get out the front door alone, had given up my career, had no money of my own, and most importantly—couldn't give up the protection he provided from my mother, who'd also been an animal killer, in her own way.

I am years from realizing that these two crucial figures in my life shared a description; more than unpredictable, they were more in pieces than the rest of us. One never knew who was in the doorway. Or what they'd bring if they came through. And yet, the three of us were in a tangle of our own kind of crazy glue, like so many others who remain ensnared until they make a run for it; children from parents and spouses and partners. But I was not a candidate for escape. I'd found my way of staying.

As many times as I'd chatted with Tessie over the garbage cans, I never let on when she wondered when her cat will return. I knew how to freeze, and that morning will remain frozen. I packed my son's toys and overalls for the flight, like those times with Bea when I'd willed myself out of the room, out of my body. Had we not had the tickets, I might have opened that box but probably not, because my terror of living alone with my child was greater than the terror of staying with his father. Being on my own with Nico was unimaginable, and imagining is how we walk through a doorway. Besides, I'd learned about reunion at my mother's knee. Years later, when l hear of a woman whose cat's throat was slit by her lover, then thrown against her as she showered, I will call myself lucky.

Departure for San Miguel was the goal, and by not looking at something too terrible to examine, we would all get on that plane. Two days later we flew to Mexico City, to my father and Clarice waiting with a cab. As we sped north from the Mexico City airport, the ochre landscape unfurled, still dusty before the July rains. Nico leaned against my chest, the buttery scent of his hair mixing with unfamiliar smells as we approached the mountains. Four hours later, all of us tired from the heat and the car's worn shocks, our driver stopped at the crest of the hill overlooking San Miguel de Allende.

"*Me amigos, por favor, Attentione!*" He exclaimed, waving his arm in a salute to his beautiful city.

Their patio lived up to my daydream, it was the safest place I'd been in years. *Park-like* was how my father had described the property he'd been so lucky to find; nearly an acre protected by the sprawling house and walls which enclosed other small buildings. For a few weeks I was home-safe, home-free, as long as I didn't corral my father into the conversation he was avoiding—the one in which I would have been asking for help.

The maid's son Jaime came every day to play with Nico. He was a few years older and protective towards his *Americano*. I watched them in the garden bent over the trucks and cars that we've brought from Brooklyn. Jaime deferred to Nico, sometimes putting his arm around his young friend's shoulder. At four, Nico chattered constantly, unaware that his Mexican playmate didn't get a single word. Jaime was a willing audience and Nico explained for both of them, as they lay face down in the spiky grass, so unlike our East coast grass. "We are resting, Mommy, because we are very tired." Nico will ignore Jaime's missing language for weeks until he defiantly announces, "Jaime is speaking Spanish, and I don't speak Spanish, but I speak to him anyway." As Nico catches on, he will say shyly to Jaime's mother, Chorna, "*adios*" or shout wildly *"gracias!"*

After a few days on the sun drenched patio, shared with birds I'd never seen before, I was released from daily adrenaline surges and ventured out of the compound alone, daring to be accountable to no one, unafraid of embarrassing myself in a foreign language. The Indian mothers sat on the curbs, nursing their babies in the folds of their *rebozos*, turning ears of corn on braziers at their feet. When a donkey was beaten to move more quickly with his load of wood, the romantic balance shifted, and I learned that this too, was Mexico.

I bought a skirt with ruffles which swirled around my ankles as I walked, saw myself in a shop window, and was startled to discover I was still pretty. I looked down at the sidewalk not because I was terrified to be outside but because cracks were everywhere and broken stones famous for San Miguel accidents. When the three of us went uptown, to El Centro, to the *Jardin*, we chose to sit with Mexicans, closer to the bandstand, and not with the *expats* who lined the front seats facing the *Paroquia* at the top of the square. I observed and, for the first time in years, could bear to be observed.

We were in one of the most sensual countries in the world, and Eckart remained distant, unless Nico crawled into his lap. My longing to be desired was inflamed by the colors, the scents, the sounds of Mexico, as if a low-grade infection had come forth and was now undeniable. But there was nothing to be done with the information, unless I was ready for the consequences.

I took a photo of Eckart, at ease in a garden chair, smiling at the camera, his handsome face as relaxed as if he'd been awakened from a dream. Not the man who'd axed the cat. Those few days he could wander for hours, on his own, without me and without Nico, who was busy with Jaime. When he'd returned, he greeted his son with bear hugs and upside-down flips, which Nico adored, his giggles echoing through the patio.

The five-minute walk from my father's house to El Centro encouraged me to come and go, come and go, as if it wasn't the big deal that it was. On my walks the bone dryness of high altitude made me feel light, my skin polished. The town was buff colored, rose, and ochre; patios linking inside and outside. For an agoraphobic this architectural detail wasn't a detail at all.

At dusk swallows streaked towards the *Belles Artes*, the eighteenth-century convent devoted to the arts, the *Jardin* filled with teenagers who walked the traditional *paseo,* when the young women walked together on the inside of the circle and the young men walked the perimeter. Long looks bridged the gap.

Without a word, like smokers or drinkers who don't announce they've quit, I began to take longer walks. With my arms filled with calla lilies, I smiled at Mexican mothers, able to meet their gaze. In Brooklyn I'd averted my eyes, but here I was free to look into their Indian faces. On the precipitous, cobbled streets, I felt safe for the first time in years but kept the information to myself, afraid to jinx it. I told myself I might even go to the open-air market to test myself in a crowd. To be on time for *comida,* the main meal of the day, I hurried along the last blocks. The days were organized around mealtimes. Clarice, somehow, managed to have Chorna duplicate her prized recipes from 23rd Street, and so we sat down to string bean casseroles and Jello salad while the strains of mariachi singers floated over the walls. My father inhaled his food as if he were still on a quick lunch break at the office, and Clarice told one of her stories without a punchline. He'd married this woman without asking himself if he liked the way she told a story. But they were far from what will become my father's disaffection and are just beginning a new life. There will be years for Clarice to decorate and redecorate the living room. When it becomes a deep ominous purple, my father will have given up his vote.

The circus was in town. Eckart and I offered to take Chorna's children. Holding as many hands as we could, we guided the kids through the throng gathered at the ticket booth. We had another child with us, a friend of Nico's, which made six in all. Coco was a year older and spoke some English. He negotiated the candy and the "cocas" and the Polaroid photos a clown took during the performance. The crude lights beamed down and the drum roll began. I heard in both languages "children of all ages" as my eyes filled with tears. The smallest boy, Adon, sat firmly on my lap. I wasn't all knotted up. I was a calm Mexican mother, my hair in a long braid; taking my six beautiful children to the circus, keeping them safe.

When the same driver pulled up to load our baggage for the return trip to the airport, my father embraced me with force as if to make up for the conversations he'd avoided. Speeding through the camel-colored land, I replayed Ted's farewell to the grandson he won't see for another year. "So long, pal. See you," he'd said, lightly tapping Nico's shoulder and abruptly turning away. As a young man, Nico will proudly hang his grandfather's luminous watercolors of fishing villages, of sun-washed barns and New York, the city Ted escaped but never got over. The paintings will be all Nico will have from this mysterious man.

Once back on Second Place, my new found bravery didn't hold. The Brooklyn streets were again dangerous, as dangerous as ever. I couldn't know yet but would learn that phobia doesn't give up without a fight—and for me, without a coach. Mornings, when Nico was in Montessori, I was working on a book that will not be published because I won't be able to tell the truth even as fiction.

Nico declared he could dress himself and began sentences with "in fact," and exclaimed "canceled" as if he meant it.

"Do cocktail parties have cupcakes?" He asked earnestly.

"Oh, I wish there weren't any people or anything that had been invented! I wish we were back with Early Man!" he murmured as he trudged upstairs, dragging his Tonka truck behind him. And one evening, very sleepy, climbing into bed, he murmured, "I can't afford a story."

Occasionally, light headed with worry, I went to a business event with Eckart but stood beside him as if he was a buoy in a storm, afraid to find the ladies room on my own. I was still turning mundane events into high drama, still standing beside my husband. We were an attractive couple, carrying as many secrets as others or maybe even more.

Late in August, a few months after those weeks in San Miguel, we were offered a few days, on our own, at a friend's farm in Vermont. Thrilled to be back again, Nico ran outside to find Mr. Woodchuck, the creature my mother named on our last visit, when I'd watched the two of them walk hand in hand down the dirt road, when I had been relieved to trust her now that he was sturdy and not the fragile baby she'd held tentatively, precariously. Now a year older, Nico raced around the familiar meadow, dizzy from rolling in the grass, bringing back dandelions wilted in his tight fist.

On those long, golden summer evenings, when our son fell quickly to sleep, there could have been time for Eckart and me, but after supper he read in a cloud of pipe smoke. I didn't dare break in, not for fear of his reaction, but fearing mine. We had gone to San Miguel just hours after he'd killed Tessie's cat in our kitchen. The cat killer was my son's father. Family wasn't *nothing*. With no way out, I had to imagine we could begin again—even be as close as we'd been when I was pregnant.

As the shadows deepened and the last of the sun burnished the meadow, before disappearing behind Mount Ascutney, I stood in the doorway, memorizing the vista, not to recreate it as my father would, but to be transported—as if the rolling, emerald panorama could magically console me, keep me safe. I didn't know then that finding comfort in vista would become a reliable totem for me—to distract from what was missing, to avoid risk.

Agoraphobia can be the cape women wrap round their shoulders, keeping them in place, at all cost. I might as well be telling you about a time as antique as Victorian England, Victorian anywhere. There were no magic pills for panic attacks, no pills that would have given me the courage to ask and then be brave enough to know whom he coveted, whom he desired.

II

10

The curved niche in the ochre wall, at the top of our staircase at Second Place, was there to accommodate a coffin and was the same as the one in the Village brownstone I'd lived in when I was ten, eleven and twelve—a Village Kid.

At ten, already the family archivist, I had pored over albums searching for clues: my father, the baby in a long white dress, unsteady on a patch of lawn, a young boy grinning in front of his camp bunk, a dashing nineteen-year-old lad arm-in-arm with his beaming parents now retired in their golden years to golden Hollywood, both he and his father striking a pose, ankles crossed, spats gleaming.

There are no photographs of my young mother or her family. Only one of her mother in a mutton sleeved blouse, her face in shadow. My mother appears in the album when she is engaged to my father. They stand amidst pines, her head on his shoulder, wrapped in smiles, leaning close. Her smile is not the strained, the pursed one to come later. Here it is open, serene. A young woman getting what she wants is how I'll see it. And I'll think that my father looks confident, as if he were making the right choice.

Theodore and Beatrice, both having changed their last names ("for professional reasons"), both getting out, leaving their immigrant parents behind, in Brooklyn and Bayonne, New Jersey. They become Ted and Bea in their new world. After my father has left her, he'll say, "your mother" only when there's trouble that I'm supposed to fix. He will delegate with a shrug, hands outstretched, helpless.

Because I have seen a photograph of my mother as a young working girl, wearing a dark suit with a white flower pinned to the lapel, I'm able to imagine the time before she met my father, when she impulsively pins a camellia to that navy suit and hops the bus to New York, filled with spunk, to get her job, to get away.

It is 1930 and she has graduated from high school and dares to head for the city, where her mother's sister Marie, who has married up, gives her a room of her own in their Riverside Drive apartment. Friday nights she returns to Bayonne, to the family house where her father still mourns her mother, dead three years, where the shades are still drawn.

As I get older, I badger my mother for pictures of her childhood, anything to put her in a world, not of imagination but of truth. I wanted to pin her down, in real rooms with curtains and cushions, like the ones my father grew up in. I wanted to know the faces of the missing grandparents just as I will, years later, try to conjure up my mother's eyes looking into mine, proof that she had seen me, her daughter, before declaring me the wrong baby.

When I insisted on information, she waved dismissively, as if to say these are unimportant details although they are the web of her life, which I knew, even then, would provide clues. The more my mother and father shrugged off their pasts, the more I imagined and invented: here they are on the Boardwalk in Atlantic City, newlyweds on a budget honeymoon, my mother's smile still as sublime as in the engagement picture. A few months after meeting, in the midst of the Depression, they married impulsively. Although they both had jobs, my father was sleeping on his married brother's couch. In the photograph my father looks like a young man dressed up for his new life, wearing his hat rakishly off-center. He sent the photo to his folks on the West coast, scrawling across the top *A COUPLE OF SWELLS SEND LOVE.*

His parents do not come east for the wedding, and my mother will store in her larder of bruised resentments, the letter from her mother-in-law which began... *I am walking down Hollywood Boulevard with tears in my eyes.* Could this have been my grandmother's Viennese operatic style and not the bullet to the heart my mother made of it? Tears of joy, I will want to believe, not the tears of regret my mother heard.

When my parents return to their West Side walk up, they can hardly get into the tiny living room. It is filled with heavy velour, a living room suite of furniture, delivered without warning and without their choosing by my mother's brother, Mac, the furniture king of Bayonne. My father, the artist, the illustrator, will give the story his spin,

"I told her to get rid of it! To call him up and get it out of there the next day! I told her it was the ugliest stuff I'd ever seen. I would not live with that garbage." He pauses, as though considering the effect on her so long ago, "I guess I embarrassed her. She went a little crazy... started screaming at me. But I was adamant. I made her call him right up, right then."

I see my mother, a few moments out of her honeymoon, forced to call this older brother, forced to refuse the gift. For a young woman, already mortified by her family, this must have been a terrible exposure... the vulgar, bulbous couch and chairs telling on her, shaming her, she of the jaunty camellia, the tentative soft smile. Still wearing her hat when she picked up that phone. I am giving her the hat in the frenzy of those moments, in the return to their new life.

Less than six months later, they will sit on a grassy knoll in Prospect Park, facing my accidental conception. My father reluctantly agrees to have this baby who has entrapped him, making it impossible to pursue his heart's desire—designing sets on Broadway. When I am eighteen and my mother is raving and shattering glassware, she will spit out the words, "I fought for you!" No one will have the wisdom to reassure me it was not *me* he didn't want or that my mother saved what was to *become* me. On that particular late summer day in Brooklyn, it was the unknown, unimagined child they argued over, not the baby girl my father insisted on naming without consulting my mother. For a guy who later presents himself as beleaguered, he was forceful in those early years.

When I arrive late in April of 1938, in an unexpected and legendary blizzard, my father isn't at my mother's side. He's out walking in Central Park when the doctor performs the emergency Caesarean. My mother's version will be that my father ran out to the park instead of staying with her. His story will be that the hours were long, the labor was mysterious, and no one told him surgery was imminent. He walked through the swirling snow to calm down, to get ready for the baby he hasn't wanted in this first year of marriage. The nurses brought me to her breast, but my mother said it hurt too much. She had them take me away. She recounts this when I'm trying to nurse my own baby after my own Caesarean, feeling the first sharp pressure and wondering how to bear this clamp of pain so that my son and I can have the pleasure, the comfort, and the health of it.

After I'm born, my father said he could never leave. Never leave me *with her*. These are the late Thirties: there was no diagnosis, no prescriptions. When she wasn't what he called *high,* she was helpless. He rushed home from the commercial art studio where, at first he was a layout man and then art director, to boil my formula for the next day. If he didn't manage the alchemy of the huge pots, the sterilization of the bottles, how would I live?

I see my petite mother in their first West 86th Street kitchen, caught in the narrow galley space, fumbling for my bottles, leaving the counter strewn with signs of meals she creates in panic. At the age of fifteen, she'd cooked for her widowed father, who'd picked and moved morsels to the edge of his plate. How could she have pleased a person so sad and silent? My mother had become a young woman in a house whose shades were drawn against the light, against the moving air. Her siblings had taken off and left her to tend to the gaunt old man, once a handsome fellow who'd cut a dignified figure, despite repeated business failures—a man in a pinstriped suit who'd lost money for decades but remained striking in the suit.

He will die of a heart attack in the subway, and my mother will tell me that she had to go by herself to identify his body because my father insisted on staying home rather than getting a sitter.

I grow and coo and find my way out of infancy. There is a blurred snapshot taken on the roof terrace of the West 86th Street apartment of me without clothes, a few steps ahead of my mother. I am unsteady, a new walker at eleven or twelve months. She's behind me, smiling, holding out an arm. Somewhere between one and two, when I walked away from her, she must have been alarmed. I am now separate and about to become my father's daughter. His childhood snapshots could be mine. Each of us with round faces and large dark eyes extolled by Uncle Manny,

"Look at those eyes! Like beautiful black olives!"

In this family, beauty was food and food was beauty... You are so adorable I could eat you up.

Between my third and fourth birthdays, there are moments so vivid I sometimes wonder if I embroidered them to animate the album, to make the movie. In this shot, my father and I sit on the studio couch with the striped bolsters, specially ordered from venerable Sloan's on Fifth Avenue. I am snug against his side, his arm around me. We are in a corner where the bookcase holds the radio and we're listening to Jack Benny on a spring evening, sunlight still streaming through the open window. We listen carefully to Benny's patter and laugh out loud together. Usually a chatterbox, I hold back for this and don't interrupt, mimicking my Daddy's laughter, not actually getting Benny's humor. My mother was not in this picture. She didn't follow this kind of delivery where every word counted. But the three of us do have a game together, started by me and turned into a real game by my father. I tiptoed into their bedroom in the early morning and squeezed between them under the covers. Before they were fully awake, I tossed back the blanket with a high pitched *Wheeee* ! My father caught on right away and gave this antic a name and with the name cooked up a game.

"EVERYONE UNDER THE TENT" he called out as if we were all far away and he was rounding us up. I found this hilarious and got instantly giddy, caught in the suspense he'd created as he covered the three of us with the blanket and then softly hissed, "EVERYONE... " and when I least expected it flung back the blanket like a sail over the bed. Without warning! That was the game, the amazing fun, to be surprised and to be warm between them.

The summer I was three they rented a house on Long Island's North Shore. It was 1941, my father's brief time designing camouflage for the Army, in Los Angeles, was over. He was back with us. A snapshot showed him sitting in a small row boat holding his fish trophy up for the camera. My mother wore a canvas hat that demurely shielded her face, and she, too, held a fish in the air. I lay on the sand, my sunburned face creased in a wide grin, warm in a white terry robe—everybody under the tent.

A few days later, I was in a shadowy hallway, trying to bring toast up the narrow stairs to my mother, who lay in bed, bleeding. I didn't know she was losing a baby. My father had gone to the city, to work, as usual. I wanted to make my mother better in that bed, and so I offered to make the toast. I went down to the kitchen and climbed onto a chair and put the bread in the slots. I knew how to push down the lever and to wait for the pop. On the steep steps I held the plate with both hands, but the toast fell off the plate, and so I retrieved the slices and blew on them carefully, and then continued up the flight. The shades in her room were drawn. It was just the two of us. There was no sound but there must have been gulls crying as they did around that house, so close to the water.

Bringing toast up a long flight of stairs in a rented summer house, when my legs are so short that the stairs might as well be a mountain trail, could be the beginning of the story of trying to make things right for my mother, of trying to fix her. The stained sheets must have been remarkable to me—years later a psychiatrist seemed to think so—but it is the scorched toast and the panicky feeling on those shadowy stairs that I remember, signaling my debut as my mother's guardian.

When I had just turned four in the spring, my parents, like many others, sent me off for the whole summer to a "Lilliputian" sleep-away camp in the Catskills. The kind of place that was *en vogue* in the Forties but will be dismantled years later when the experts realize it is not such a good idea to send such little ones away for the whole summer.

After Lights Out in our bunk, I lay curled on my cot, hugging my knees and sniffling with longing. The counselor couldn't dissuade me from my nightly ritual of crying for home, for 10th Street, for my room with the circus wallpaper, for Everybody Under The Tent. Although I cried myself to sleep at night, during the day I was given the grown-up job of riding unsaddled horses. Put the ponies to sleep in the barn, the riding instructor told me, giving me the most power I'd ever known. The ponies could as well be large dogs on leashes like the ones in Washington Square Park where I was longing to be, except on those late afternoons when I did my job. Fearful of deep water in the pool, I was fearless on the mare's glistening back. I held onto her tangled mane as we rocked towards the gate: a four-year-old girl riding bareback without a helmet in 1942.

Now I can adjust the lens of that summer and see that tiny girl atop the mare, staring straight into the camera, still homesick but grinning with pride, more brave than lost.

11

My parents were inadvertent Villagers, not intentional Bohemians seeking the Village of rebellion. We ended up on 10th Street because my mother's older sister, Lil, lived on the block with her boys and her husband, Mike, a Jew from Oklahoma who wore a felt cowboy hat in all weather and did publicity for RKO Pictures, a great talker, married to a woman who was mostly silent and who will keep her distance from my mother when things get really bad. Their son Stephan went to The Little Red School House. Although PS 41 was just across Sixth Avenue on Greenwich Avenue, my mother got my father to pay for me to go to Little Red despite his Depression fears about money that will haunt him forever.

The Whitney Museum on 8th Street was a place for me and my mother to pop into on a rainy day or on the way home after school. Her arms filled with packages and my jaws aching from the Double Bubble given as a treat and a lure for the artistic detour she wanted. Close to her side, I chattered my way up 8th Street, past Womrath's bookstore, Gristedes (fine foods), the jewelry stores, the framer, and the Chinese restaurant, telling her about school, about dodgeball, about being quick, about not getting *out* and how the art teacher sent me out of the room for talking. For Talking!

"Pearl pinched my arm, really pinched when she took me out of Art. (We called all our teachers by first name at The Little Red School House.) She's a boss, a real meaney."

I tugged at her sleeve to see if she was listening. It was an automatic tug. I didn't expect to get her attention. I ran on like a radio.

"What's wrong with talking and painting? And the lunch was yucky anyway..."

I can't know then that my yearning for her attention will keep me coming back, no matter what; that no price was too high for her attention, which I must have equated with love—never reliable, always a promise. If only I could decipher the code.

As we climbed the marble staircase of the old Whitney mansion, I prattled more softly and became quiet under the gauzy haze streaming through the skylights. We were often the only two people in the gallery. The silence, the soft light and not getting her attention made me feel lonely, but because she seemed calm I was also relieved. Moving from one painting to another, I was with the gentle, distracted mother, not the one who could suddenly fly at me. Or grab my box of crayons, throwing them to the floor in a rage. Or leave the bathroom, her robe unbuttoned, a sanitary pad in clear view. Rain was *beat beat beating* on the skylights of that still room. She seemed to have disappeared into the canvases although she won't become a painter until I'm in high school. She stared at the pictures as she will, years later, when clinically depressed, nearly catatonic, disappear into a mirror for hours. As the Double Bubble treat spread sugary comfort across my tongue, I ran circles round the room just for fun, to break the dreamy silence, to have one of those seductive moments that never lasted—when she suddenly smiled at me before vanishing again. I didn't know that I longed for her true company.

My 10th Street was as still, in the early forties, as one of Edward Hopper's streets. The sun hit the north side of our block in the afternoon, when the facades were burnished deep chocolate and dusty red. Our dachshund, Cokey, was walked in that sunlight. I see her now burnished as well. She was a little seal of a dog, leading me up the street as my mother trailed behind. I want to think my mother knew how powerful it was for me holding that leash as Cokey pulled me along and me, holding tight, in charge. But did she have to tell me that Cokey had been pelted with stones for being a German dog, by some tough boys who ran away? I was learning to expect the unexpected. To sleep with one eye open.

In the evening, when I most missed my Dad, who was in Los Angeles, in some misplaced whacky jab at cheerfulness, she pretended to be Daddy, flapping around the room, like a silly bird, making both of us giggle at the sight of my tiny mother in his big striped pajamas. "Everyone Under The Tent!" I screeched to start the game I loved, invented by the Daddy I was missing. But perhaps because the game was too much his invention and would have brought me to tears, not giggles, she refused to play that one. "It's too late. No more games, time to sleep."

Although I was four, we agreed to pretend I was a baby, ready for her rendition of Brahms' lullaby. I lay on my stomach in the dark and felt her hand lightly patting my back, as she hummed in her perfectly pitched voice. This was not the crazy voice that snarled or rose in gasps of rage or will be destroyed by Thorazine, years later, when she is psychotic. This was the soft lilting of the other woman, the other mother. As she patted my back in tentative irregular beats, she also touched my hair so lightly that I couldn't be sure it was her hand, but when I'm grown and even middle-aged, a light touch on the back of my head, ruffling my hair, can bring me to tears.

When she closed the door, and I saw the hall light, I pretended to be asleep so that she'd know she'd been the good mother, the one who's put me to sleep with her singing. I didn't expect the snarling mother to reappear because I still believed that scary woman was accidental and that the soft mother was the real one, the one who might be there in the morning. I was four and could give my mother the benefit of the doubt.

When we moved to the West Village, she and I walked home from The Little Red School House along Bleecker Street, its curb lined with pushcarts. We passed shop windows with hanging cheeses and salamis. I was fascinated by the salted cod, which smelled of the sea although the wooden floor was strewn with sawdust. Years later, marooned in Carroll Gardens, the same scent of cheese and sawdust in Frank's corner store will fill me with longing for my Bleecker Street and for that jaunty, spunky girl darting amongst the pushcarts as the Italian housewives leaned over vegetables, murmuring and squeezing. Despite the astonishing choice of fresh produce, my mother was in the grip of an American love affair with canned or frozen food. She was first-generation—the ones who have gotten away, opened cans, defrosted.

After Bleecker Street, we headed over to Washington Square Park and then to 8th Street to shop at Gristedes, my mother's club, the long-suffering Irish clerks, in long white aprons, her personal staff. Having lost her list, she would stand at the marble counter as the clerk ran back and forth, filling her order to be delivered to our apartment.

Daily life took place below 14th Street. We only go uptown to see doctors; to get Mary Janes and haircuts at Best's on 5th Avenue. The double-decker bus connected us to uptown events, winding us back and forth on the ribbon of 5th Avenue, ending at the Arch, the entrance to Washington Square Park.

It was on the 5th Avenue bus that my mother's cheeks would become flushed. She would clutch her packages and steer me to a seat with a rough push, hissing words I couldn't make out… about the air, the heat, someone's elbow. Her breathing was fast, her teeth were clenched, and I wasn't sure why there was so much trouble, but I knew trouble when I saw it. Regular mothers didn't get the attention that mine got. I wish no one would look at us; just being noticed felt dangerous. In that crowded, swerving bus I wanted to quiet her down, smooth her out and make her mind her business: this unruly, boiling coffee pot of a mother, not to be trusted, who could burst into my room when I'm playing with a friend, throw open my door, rage in, wearing a short smock revealing a Kotex dangling between her legs. I don't remember how many times this happened. The bloody napkin is what remains.

Every Friday the three of us went out for supper at the Greek restaurant on our corner. The Athens could have been one of Edward Hopper's restaurants. It was there, in April of 1944, that the radio music stopped to announce President Roosevelt's death. As the sun streamed in across Sixth Avenue, our waiter stood motionless, his towel tucked over his arm, like one in a Hopper painting. My father's eyes filled with tears for the first and only time I will remember. I was six years old and knew something important had happened. Even my mother was paying attention.

Most of those evenings, I skipped out of The Athens with my Napoleon dessert and sped past my parents to the florist, where I traded my dessert for a rose. By the time my parents sauntered up the block, I'd completed my transaction and was flushed with the excitement of deal-making.

We headed for home, around the corner to 10th Street, making a swell picture of a small family as we entered the building, my parents nodding to the doorman. My sweaters were always red, bright cheerful red, and my mother almost always wore British Brevets, those gleaming brogues of hers. The weather was fine and the early evening light still in the sky, as the doorman saw a unit of three ascending to their proper apartment.

Private school must have been a hard-won victory for my mother. I like to think that she stood up for me and enrolled me in The Little Red Schoolhouse, just as she stood up to my father about the Christmas tree in the winter. I'm seven and Janie Brodman is my best friend. Janie's parents were Jews who cared about being Jewish, not like my parents who changed their names and ironed themselves out. We'd always had a Christmas tree so when my father mysteriously announced no tree for that Christmas, I was crushed. My mother took my part and argued for the tree but then gave in, and I went off to bed with a dramatic flounce.

The next day as we walked down 8th Street at dusk, with shop lights casting color on the hard-packed snow, my mother impulsively stopped and bought a small fat spruce. They were at the curb every year, only this time my father wasn't with us to carry it home across his shoulder. She paid quickly as if she was buying on the black market and told me to pick up the trunk as she lifted the middle.

We continued down the block, with me struggling to hold up my end of the tree, and other shoppers making room for us just as Janie's mother, Mrs. Brodman, suddenly appeared, beaming and greeting us in her accented English. My mother smiled back, grasping the tree trunk with a gloved hand and blithely behaving as if there was no tree bobbing behind her, and no small girl hanging on to the trunk, her mittens sticky with sap. I didn't say a word. I was in awe of my mother's performance, to get the tree, to stand up to my father, and now to face Mrs. Brodman red-handed. At that moment, I became her co-conspirator in the Christmas Tree Plot. It was one of those times when my mother's craziness became zaniness and might be called "plucky." My usual embarrassment was replaced with glee, with sheer excitement for her daring.

That same year we sat side by side on red velvet, in darkness, two secret hooky players at the Loew's movie theater on Greenwich Avenue. On those afternoon matinees, we were in perfect collaboration, conspirators against the workaday world of homework, housework. Each time, there was the exquisite pleasure of dimming lights and the crackle of cellophane as I opened the chewy jelly box of Dots: the moment of transport, out of this world, into the movie—me and my mom and Betty Grable.

As we raised our faces to the screen, I grinned and leaned into her shoulder. She smiled back, her face lit by amazing Technicolor, and took my hand. 8th Street and the Christmas tree and Loew's Sheridan will live forever in the Good Enough Mother Album, enlarged and exaggerated whenever I needed her, needed to believe I'd been the daughter she'd wanted, despite growing evidence to the contrary.

Watercolor was my father's medium. As he drew with bold strokes, I hung around the drawing board, circling him with questions. He was the parent who might answer. When he'd brought work home from the office, he blocked out a layout while my mother sulked in the kitchen, in the midst of her clutter, "whipping" up Sunday dinner.

There was a palpable sadness in those Sunday afternoons, the scent of disappointment in the air, as if, once more, the weekend hadn't brought what anyone wanted. I could be found sitting on the floor with Cokey curled in my lap. My father's friend Terry, also an artist, captured this moment on canvas, painting us as if we're joined, my arms cradling the small black dog. Years after the painting is lost, I can see its chrome yellow background, making Cokey safe in my lap, making me safe.

My mother's one real pal seemed to be my friend Susie's mother, Sarah. When the two women sat in Sarah's sunny kitchen, drinking tea and nibbling pastries, the tumble of Sarah's handbag business—leather and tools mixed in the sunlit kitchen with spices and vegetables—felt natural to me, the Village kid. In that swirl of food and handicraft, it seemed my mother was glad to be there with Sarah. I was secretly happy my mother had a friend, too. I was nine and had not yet taken up my teenage *lorgnette* that will tell me what is conventional and desirable or what is off-beat and suspect. I have not yet dumped Susie.

In 1949, after a year in a ranch house in North Hollywood, where I watched tumble-weed roll down our street and discovered, when taunted by the tow-headed girls next door, that *kike* meant *Jew*, we returned to the Village. We'd come home from what my mother referred to as "the godforsaken San Fernando Valley." Years later, she'll tell me we'd moved there so that my father didn't have to witness his older brother's futile battle with cancer. She will describe his decision without any sympathy for my father's terror of illness, for his lack of courage in the face of it. More years later, I will wonder if she even knew that his beloved Grandma Rosa had suffered the pain of breast cancer, at their house in Flatbush, with nothing for pain, and her mysterious disappearance into an ambulance, never to be seen again by my eight-year-old father. I will also wonder, if Bea knew, did it mean anything to her? And could she possibly connect his fear to what was happening to her? No one signs up for mental illness in the family, but my father was not the one for this job.

Apartments were scarce after the war, and we were lucky to get one in the South Village. On Charlton Street, a block from Varick Street's industrial buildings, our floor through caught the odd waft of printer's ink and baking bread. The brownstone was built on land rumored to have belonged to the infamous traitor Aaron Burr, which will mean something to me years later, when I want to claim residency in such a house, as if a distinguished house could reframe the story, make it nice. A replacement for the picket fence family I was longing for.

Levita, our rotund West Indian cleaning lady, moved ever so slowly through the apartment; her sing-song accent soothing my mother, heading off an outburst. She taught me to pad as softly as she did, to wait for explosions to wind down. She put an index finger to her lips, giving me the sign to come to the darkened room where my mother lies, her arm across her face, her mouth pursed, the flood of words finally damned. Only then am I to say, "Would you like some water? What about some tea?" I stood motionless, in the doorway, hoping my tone was okay, my words nonflammable, in training for the job of managing the unmanageable.

It was a summer day, and in summer things were worse. The heat seemed to enter my mother and boil around. She didn't breathe like other people. Caught in her own battle with the close air, her finger jabbed at my arm, propelling me towards the front door. I longed for it to be cooler, for a breeze. Had I made my mother crazy again?

"Find the damned keys for me . . . " She hissed between clenched teeth, as she stood at the hall table, fumbling in her purse. She dumped the contents onto the table in desperation, as if the train was leaving. Just getting out the door could be a dangerous event. I imagined we might fall right down the dimly lit staircase, but we made it to the street. As we started up 6th Avenue, she veered off towards the Good Humor truck.

"I don't feel like one now." I said. For an instant, she looked at me and smiled, absently, like someone finding their place in a text.

I knew that smile was the way out of this trouble, and so I accepted the cone and its cool comfort, after all.

Kitchen drama was created every night. My mother's cheeks flushed with panic, and my father's face set in resignation. He loved food and never got used to the evening's disappointment. She, in turn, hurried the preparation in some misplaced belief that if the lamb chops were served just as he hung up his coat, it will be a sign that she was waiting for him, that the carelessly cooked lamb (never gray enough for him) would make a bridge between them. But this rush to the table always backfired, putting her in the hot seat, defending the pink lamb.

On the weekends, my father, a reliable but unimaginative cook, showed me some basic recipes. As he and I layered tuna casseroles and munched potato chips, which will dissolve in the Campbell's soup, we nearly whistled while we worked, my mother exiled to the living room where she read and smoked, stubbing out cigarettes after one or two puffs, lighting another. Was she relieved to be out of the job, or was she jealous of the bond between us?

By the time I was thirteen, I longed even more for an unremarkable, unnoticeable Mother. I was beginning to see how our Village life will not mesh with my Uptown notions of regular families. I now had Uptown girlfriends and went to sleepovers in their Central Park West apartments, where cooks served dinner and no one got up from the table until the meal was over.

I dreamt of an apartment that didn't flow through to a makeshift kitchen, devised from a former sun porch, where meals were made calmly, eaten calmly. I took up my father's call for a place for everything. Without intending to ambush her, but just by being more at home with the kitchen arsenal, I was becoming her enemy. "Mom... I smell something." I pointed to the seething oven. Smoke was escaping round the edges of its door. The delicious scent of broiling had become an emergency.

Startled, as if awakened, my mother pulled the chops from the flames. "Take your chops! Too hot, too hot in here! " She shrieked at the stove as if it were alive, coming for her. The kitchen was, in fact, narrow and close with oven heat. She was trapped in enemy territory. "I try... you two bastards... no one knows, no one knows,... " she moaned as she jammed ruffled paper panties onto the bones.

If we dared to break in, the crescendo built until she tore at her blouse, splitting the silk. This tearing of her blouse, its sleeves yanked from shoulder seams, frightened me more than any dish flying across the room. Those blouses, from Lord & Taylor, had been carried home in bright packages after her hair was shampooed, her cheeks still pink from the dryer at the salon. On those afternoons, there was a kind of calm, even a truce in her battles with panic, disorder, and her daughter.

When something was right—the temperature of her tea or my brushing her hair rhythmically as her face tilted back in a swoon—I was relieved at giving her *relief.* When those same blouses hung off her brassiere, tossed back from her soft shoulders, scraps of rosy silk against her skin, my throat tightened. There was too much skin. Would the whole brassiere be torn off as her nipples appeared in the dining room?

My father flung down his napkin, heading for the television set, another of her enemies. The abandoned lamb would be there in the morning, congealed, accusative.

It was easy in the Village days of the Forties and Fifties to confuse madness with eccentricity; in that leftover Bohemian atmosphere, sketchy housekeeping and derelict kitchen habits would never be called *thought disorder*. Off-hand charm abounded. Even my friends' kitchens were disheveled, in cheerful disarray. Against this backdrop of neighborhood characters, my mother cut a nearly bourgeois figure in her Lord & Taylor tweeds, gleaming brogues, and dusty tea rose lipstick and polish, the ladylike color that will become false to me when I know those lips can grimace, those nails can scratch.

In my mother's movie, she *rolled with the punches, put on her face, had mad money*, got back her *land legs,* and always wore a *fetching* hat. No one will foresee midnight ambulance rides, her arms strapped to her sides, her voice barking and gagging, me crouched on a folding seat as the ambulance swerves its way to a Westchester madhouse that I will dutifully visit—my terror of being *like* her mixed up with my guilt of being *not* like her. And yet, still fiercely loyal to *before . . .* to the three of us digging into sandwiches on plaid picnic blankets, to Cokey, the dachie, sniffing happily, and my mother as dreamy as she was in their engagement snapshot, leaning against my father, beneath the feathery pines.

III

12

When we left the Village and moved Uptown, I was sixteen, had discovered Virginia Woolf, had found an ally even though Woolf's heroines had an Edwardian household to protect them with velvet drapes and paisley shawls. The English writer was a delicate, demanding woman with an imagination that would eventually succumb to madness and suicide.

I won't know for a long time that Woolf's illness had the same name as my mother's. I will, in later years, be mortified to realize that whereas Woolf was cosseted and held in her husband Leonard's caring embrace, my mother was tossed into ambulances and strapped down for electroshock treatments without her husband by her side. Separated by class and culture, she shared only a diagnosis with the privileged, doomed writer. Woolf's taking her own life was another distinction. Bea's despair propelled on others.

Because the Charlton Street brownstone in the Village had been sold and there was no time for a search, we moved to a one-bedroom apartment on West 77th Street where I was given the bedroom and my parents slept on studio couches in the living room, overlooking The American Museum of Natural History. This sleeping arrangement was likely a signal of the change in their relationship. I must have noticed this but at fifteen, I was more focused on me, not them.

I'd been a Village girl, used to narrow spaces, crooked corners, but now I had to navigate broad bands of streets. My mother never commented on this new terrain, and I wondered when I became agoraphobic if the wide proportions of our 77th Street had troubled *her*. By then I will be afraid I've inherited lots more than her amazing sense of color.

In this new neighborhood we had a new dog to replace both Cokey and then Penny who've died young, from mysterious stomach ailments. I was never told exactly what happened to them, but somehow I attributed their deaths to my mother. The chaotic kitchen counters, the cleansers that were never capped under the sink, and how she'd rushed to get me the new blond cocker puppy, Buffy, who arrived against my father's wishes, like the Christmas tree that winter when my mother defied him. It was one of those times with her I'll embroider, not just to be fair but because I need them.

I could no longer race up the stoop of the brownstone, fly into the dimly lit hallway, and open a door, which, even in 1955, was left unlocked. Now the elevator was often crowded, the air stuffy in this building with many tenants. Buffy, a snappish cocker, was held on a short leash. The small elevator was like being on the bus with my mother. At any moment her stream of consciousness could flow. What fascinated in Woolf's voice—now mortified me.

"... the doorman, that bozo... never there when needed..." My mother looked so normal and began with something anyone could relate to, but when she moved into a rant, "... a charming hat... mad money that's the ticket... I held the fort," folks looked away, studied their shoes or fumbled with keys, waiting for the sliding door to set them free. This was worse than being little and being on the bus with her. Now I was humiliated not bewildered. I heard this garbled talk and moved away, pretending not to know her. I won't be her daughter in the elevator or any other place where she exposed herself. In that small space, with her cheeks flushed, her eyes darting for any kind of contact, she could just as well be tearing off her blouse.

Now that the Village could no longer protect her, she was more on display in the new setting and will be found out. Already given to magical thinking, it seemed to me if my mother had stayed downtown, on those cozy crooked streets, she might have blended in with the other eccentric Village characters I'd known all my life. And not draw all the wrong attention. I was a girl of sixteen confusing wrong attention with expression as if they have the same effect; being noticed was linked with being out of control. I was watching my step, lowering my voice.

Out of the Village, but still in Elisabeth Irwin High School, to which I will travel for one last year, going downtown on the subway was a big deal. On the A train, on the way to school, I sometimes thought of my grandfather dying of a heart attack on a subway platform. I had no real memory of this man, who visited us at the 10th Street apartment but remained shadowy except in his exceptional death. I had to take the spooky subway to get back to the Village, so that I could graduate and get away.

Every morning I met the boys from my class. They nobly held open the doors of the train. Most of them were from prominent families. Their fathers had inherited radio networks, brokerage firms, and family businesses, and their mothers told cooks what to prepare for dinner. These guys wore camel hair coats instead of the team basketball jackets like the Village boys and behaved as if their penises were made of cashmere. They seemed to feel entitled in ways that the Downtown guys didn't. I was not actually familiar with their penises. I just felt them through their pants as we swayed in the gym ballroom at the monthly dances. I'd not yet seen a real penis and was both confused and intrigued by the insistent probe against my skirt. It could as well be a small animal caught between us, trapped and pressing for release. Even when the music stopped, we clung to each other surrounded by the pungent waft of gym sweat.

When we'd been living Downtown, I dreamed of Uptown and all it promised; now that I was Uptown, I modeled myself as an expatriate, someone just passing through. I was uneasy and animated, fearful and wildly fantasizing, trying to make my way through the web of high school. Years later, I would see myself as a displaced Bohemian, wrapping myself in Indian shawls, instead of navy cardigans, unaware that Someplace Else had become a permanent habitat.

My summer camp friend, Marcy, fueled this particular fire of displacement. She'd spent a few post-war years in the South of France and in Berlin, where she struck black market deals with German kids, trading her parent's cigarettes for chocolate. She lived in faded villas with overgrown gardens and *au pairs* who left Marcy and her sister to wander the neighborhood, while their parents assumed the girls were safe. Marcy urged me on in our dreamy schemes: together we dyed stockings in her bathtub, never really getting the tub white again, trying for indescribable jewels of lavender, emerald and cognac. Her schoolteacher mother appeared at the bathroom door and peered over the edge of the tub to inspect our efforts and to remind us, without conviction, to clean up after ourselves, to be sure to scrub the tub. She murmured these instructions softly, distractedly. A retiring figure with amber beads and upswept dyed hair, she was a preoccupied woman who left us to do as we pleased but also the mother who prepared dinner and preferred to do so without any help.

Both emerging from our baby fat, Marcy and I were otherwise, true opposites. She had thick, dirty blond hair and hazel eyes, my dark coffee brown hair matched my eyes. We mimicked each other as we arched our necks and dilated our nostrils, affecting a kind of mid-Atlantic accent designed to make people ask if we were American born. In addition to a mutual hatred for our camp counselor, we shared a fascination with things *European.*

Just before we met at camp in the Catskills, I'd been on my first trip to Europe with my parents. One evening in Geneva my mother had my father and me laughing hysterically as she danced around the room in her pajamas imitating the Swiss chamber maid. The next morning, my father packed her suitcase as he always did, to make sure she was ready, to make sure she could keep up with us. It seemed he did it in good spirits then and without the terse closed mouth he had when he picked up after her at home.

After the summer and now fast friends, Marcy proposed a trip to the Bonwit Teller lingerie department, where in the dressing room she dared to pull on two satin slips beneath her skirt. Already an experienced shoplifter, she guided me, weak-kneed, to the elevator and then onto Fifth Avenue where we collapsed into high hilarity.

"Oh my God, I thought you were kidding! You did it, you actually did it!" I was pale with fear and sure we'll be yanked back into the store where we'll be arrested. I gasped. "You're crazy, really crazy!"

Shrugging, she headed purposefully up Fifth, just another New Yorker in a hurry. I sprinted to keep up as she turned back to smile triumphantly and put her arm through mine.

"It was nothing. I didn't want to shock you, so I just took two, it could have been five or six!" She paused for effect, smirking like when she told the black market stories. It was intoxicating, to have witnessed the crime and then to be safe, out in the sunshine, with my new best friend.

Becoming friends with Marcy created a kind of a bridge between my new Uptown life and the Village we'd left behind. The Weimans were like the families from Downtown: their walls filled with art and African masks. Our parents got together occasionally, and her mother met mine for lunch. The best part of all was that my mother let me have my friend and didn't barge into my room when we were supposed to be doing homework but were deep in rambling talk. Because she had Mrs.Weiman, I didn't have to worry about my mother's interruptions.

Although I never dared repeat the Bonwit performance, I wanted to be daring in my own way. I took Marcy to the West Side piers, to go aboard *The Liberté*, to spy together on the jaunty French sailor, in the tight britches, who had flirted with me mercilessly all the way home across the Atlantic. Those days at sea, I'd found every excuse to prowl the decks, until I found him hoisting a cable, polishing a brass fitting. He'd wait until I was mortified to be discovered and then suddenly he'd turn and grin, the conspiratorial grin which bound me to him, as if we were actually entwined.

We were far from entwined and on the whole crossing spoke only a few words.

"*Êtes-vous Américain?*" It was enchanting to even be *asked* if I was American.

"*Oui, bien sûr,*" I replied, caught in his meaningful gaze. His dark almond eyes suited my purposes better than clear blue ones. I've already decided that light eyes didn't allow for submersion, for the kind of mystery I was after.

Paul Vallé was eighteen and the oldest boy to capture my attention. We never touched and never spoke more than my first-year French would permit. I never wished for more language, which was astonishing for a girl who had been chattering most of her young life. Paul promised that when the ship returned to New York, we would see each other. I was sure we would progress. I was well into the business of making things up. I kept his eyes and high flushed cheek bones, the swagger of him intact and retrievable—a delightful package to be opened and reopened. I was learning to memorize my lover's face long before I would have one.

Such was the power of those few days at sea that for months I checked *The New York Times* for his arrival, peering at the columns like an old investor timing the market. Marcy, having felt like an outsider on her return from Germany, was primed for these capers. My new obsession and fascination with things European, was sealing our friendship. We now shared a common purpose, much more powerful than just not liking camp; we distained the ordinary, the available, and pursued the elusive. Without ever using the word Bohemian, we were beguiled by whatever we deemed to be un-American.

We made several visits to the ship and went aboard as visitors could, but only saw Paul once and he was not the same, with Marcy as witness. He nodded in our direction and returned to polishing. She was baffled. "He's gorgeous. You didn't exaggerate. But he ignored you!" I didn't admit that secretly I was relieved that apart from this one actual non-reunion, it was almost better not to see him—just to track him was the point. He would never be my dancing partner, would not press against me in the sweaty gym, but he made my high school boys look pale, and gave me the edge I needed—to hold myself apart, to stand in the doorway instead of coming into the room.

One of the pleasures of being in high school was being able to move around the city on my own. I walked up 6th Avenue to 12th Street to visit with my Grandma Tess who'd sent the perfect skirts and vests, the buttery cookies. After Grandpa Herman's sudden death in Hollywood, she was back in New York, making a fuss over me.

As soon as she buzzed me into the vestibule, I was happy to climb the stairs and to know that with the door wide open, she waited to hold me in her snug embrace.

"*Ach du lieber Gott, so schoen, so schoen...*" I was beautiful, just for being there.

The table was set before the window overlooking the street. Familiar heart shaped cookies, the Sanka she preferred to tea, and usually a surprise a tiny velvet box or colored tissue holding a pin, a decorated barrette, a costume ring she'd found on her 14th Street expeditions because she was still fit enough, at eighty, to traipse for hours, to climb the flights home, and to relish her evenings with no one expecting a meal. Her widowhood was a release, and the nostalgic stories of my Grandpa Herman will come when I'm in college, Grandma in her late 80s, and the past has become her only present.

"Tell me, tell me," she began after our first cup.

I regaled her with my latest classroom triumph she may understand. Her schooling stopped at fourteen in Vienna but she had memorized Heinrich Heine and wanted me to know that. Her own son, my father, had never heard Heine's stanzas, had never heard the shipboard story.

"You see, *meine susse*, we changed train stations and so, in Berlin, my mama walked us through the Brandenburger Tor at midnight, and we took the train to Hamburg and there we found the ship... I was the oldest, but only fourteen. You know, I was really very pretty and we were in steerage (these two facts seemed connected for her) and one day, the doctor, the young doctor with hair as red as mine saw me on the deck and that was that... he brought me oranges for the family each day. We said only a few words, but in the morning we looked into each other's eyes, when I took those oranges, and then he'd be gone and I'd have to go below."

I didn't yet know what steerage was but when I do, I'll see her descending the stairs as the stench rises.

She sighed looking out onto 12th Street, her hand on mine.

"So, so we docked. *meine vater*, who will die in a very few months, comes for us. I never see the beautiful doctor again. And I never forget him."

When I wasn't enthralled with the pursuit of Eros, I was drawn to our school productions, sometimes acting or on the set design crew, proud to be painting scenery with my Dad, who volunteered to bring our productions up to snuff and who seemed happy to be back in a world he'd left when he married my mother and became a father all too soon. The illusion he created with a few brush strokes dazzled our crew for *Finian's Rainbow.* As he drew and painted, they stood quietly behind him.

"It's all pretty simple," he said as he swept his brush across the construction paper. The kids were mesmerized. This was the presentable, even trustworthy, parent in public, not only engaging but talented, a person with something others valued. I would learn, in a few years, what this currency of his will cost me.

Evenings and weekends were taken up with mixing color, stretching large sheets of brown paper across two by fours to create a backdrop, learning to choose the amazing gels that change the light that spilled onto the actors' faces transforming the most stolid features into the mysterious. I'll soon be obsessed with vista, a color to wash a wall, a hunk of velvet across a nasty sofa—as if setting was what I could control no matter what. "Stop rearranging your room, arrange your life!" my father would taunt as he passed my room and saw the bed and dresser, moved yet again.

When we painted the brown paper and shared sandwiches with the theater kids, we were leaving my mother out, once again having a good time by ourselves.

"I feel bad that Mom's by herself… Think she's o.k.?" I asked with my head bent over the scenery, the worry all mine.

"For God's sake, what does she have to do with this? She'd just be in the way."

My worry was lifted when, with my father's encouragement, my mother ventured to the Art Student's League on 57th Street, and found teachers who discovered her talent. Her first still life, dusty yellow mums in an earthenware jar, will be one of her best works even as her palette becomes more daring. She, who couldn't organize her kitchen, could organize a painting. She won praise from her classmates, from her instructors, and for a brief time, from my father. (After he has left her, he will call her work *accidental*.) It was such a relief for her to be at the League, that sometimes we started cooking without her. We laughed as we chopped and mixed and listened to my favorite record, *Oklahoma*. When she got home, her hands smudged with paint, she was glowing as she showed off her latest canvas. Her face was flushed, not with the usual kitchen panic but with pride. My father praised her paintings extravagantly, propped them in a place of honor, and then presented our casserole with a flourish. I saw that it might be possible—that my mother could be happy, and that I could give up the watch—until I couldn't.

The summer following my obsession with my French sailor I was off to camp as a counselor in training: back to the Catskills, back to meadows where the small girl had been steady holding the reins as the mare circled the paddock. Now the scent of hay surrounded me as I lay against the bales with Scott, the farmer's son, who drove the tractor at our camp. Here, too, there was a language barrier. The city mouse spoke *city* while the country mouse said even less than the Frenchman did. I sat behind him on the tractor, my arms around his bare chest, his scent of sun and sweat. When we rubbed against each other's dungarees, pleasure and fear were joined. I was still free to imagine, but with more information. What had only been my grandmother's croon, *meine susse, meine susse,* will now be whispered endearments by guys who want something and who get me to want it, too.

When the summer was over, I returned to school and to my city boys. My parents were as mysterious as ever, but I was less and less interested in them.

The search for a graduation dress was on. My mother and I were revisiting the scenes of so many dressing room dramas at Lord & Taylor. It was in these small, stuffy cubicles that she had been at her worst, not admitting to claustrophobia but instead rifling through my choices angrily, hurriedly, pressing for choices teenagers can't make without excruciating deliberation. As I waffled indecisively, my mother boiled. This choice was the most important in my short history, for here I will present myself, not only to my classmates but to a larger audience, parents, the world. I traced my finger across the lawn batiste, the filmy whiteness. Small raised rose buds were strewn, as if fallen, onto the cloth.

"This is it, don't you think?" I searched her face for the endorsement I still needed even after years of dyeing stockings with Wendy and declaring ourselves immune to taste that wasn't ours.

She'd taken off her tweed jacket and was crossing and recrossing her shapely ankles, the straps of her British Brevits accenting her high instep. Distracted, searching her purse for a cigarette, she snapped,

"Whatever... Take it! Get out of here... too hot, too damn hot!"

She told me to move it—to get out of the perfect dress and to meet her at the desk where I'll be mortified as the sales lady sized up my mother and handed me the package without looking at either of us.

Our new apartment on West End Avenue was a more normal arrangement than 79th Street. There were two bedrooms and a bath and a half. My father, the artist now an advertising guy, exclaimed that with the former tenant's beige carpet a*nd* the smoked mirrors, we'd arrived at wall-to-wall boredom! I was standing in front of these mirrors to model my dress for my father. As usual, he didn't comment on me but did approve the dress.

"It's a knockout," he said, lighting his pipe and turning too quickly away.

Pals in the kitchen, pals at the school play, he still couldn't take part in the tribal father-daughter contract. Permission to be a *femme fatale* will not come from him. But on the night of graduation, he backed me up.

It was one of those balmy June evenings, when New York has a waft of its sultry summers. The air in the apartment was close. My mother had been in the steamy bathroom for a long time. I stayed clear of the closed door and tried without success to smooth the long satin sash of my perfect dress. I knew better than to rap on the door and ask her to iron it. I knew how to iron but was teary with panic and the picture of imperfection that loomed for the evening. My father stood in the doorway in his blue serge suit.

Quickly removing his jacket he said, "I can do it. Get the iron. I can do this in two minutes."

We heard the slamming of the bathroom cabinet, my mother's mutterings punctuated with Goddamns. As he glided the iron back and forth across the satin, he reminisced as if this was just an ordinary night,

"When I was a kid I made marionettes in our basement in Flatbush... just before the show Grandma ironed the costumes with me. She'd stitch them by hand." He's slowed me down, quieted the beat in my temples.

As I fastened the sash around my waist I chimed in, "Grandma still says, 'Anything my eyes can see, my hands can make,'" taking my cue from him, as my mother's voice came from the bathroom: ". .. heat... no time... white gloves."

This evening was not a cozy assembly. The principal will call out our names. Carried on waves of "Where e're You Walk," I moved carefully down the aisle towards the stage where we'd performed our beloved *Finian's Rainbow*.

I scanned the aisles to find my parents, and grinned at my father who was smiling at me, his infectious I-can-sell-you-the-Brooklyn Bridge smile. I tried to catch my mother's eye, but she was staring into her compact, adjusting the veil of her fetching hat.

13

Choosing Sarah Lawrence and not the University of Michigan kept me close to Manhattan—and too close to my parents. As it would turn out, the forty-five minute train ride to Bronxville was never enough time to shake off the effects of a visit home. But arriving back at the campus and Westland's gate was crossing to safety. Brick walks, Tudor dorms, velvet lawns held us in an embrace. Our only job was to read and write and think in ways that would lead us to our true selves.

Conferences with "Dons" were intense; accomplished professors hung on our every word. The rarest of blooms, growing in the hothouse of the most expensive college in the country, we stayed awake into the night, debating existentialism, virginity, and other urgent issues. Flushed with excitement—it was 1956, and we were still post-war Fifties girls.

I started behaving as if I wanted something. I had pals up and down the corridor, where the telephone was located, but it didn't occur to me that my mother would use the telephone like a missile. It also didn't occur to me to ignore her daily messages, her pleas and ramblings, and peppered throughout, her implication that I'd abandoned her.

Returning from a French lit class, in which the seductive, much-married professor had proclaimed that as we studied *Madame Bovary* I resembled her more and more, I was stopped in my elated tracks by a note pinned to my door: "Call your Mom, Important."

"Hi, are you okay?" I said, closing my eyes.

"Am I okay? Is that what I get? I've been trying you all morning!" Her voice rose, heading for the register that froze me.

"Sorry, sorry... I have early classes... what's happening?" My throat closed as if she was standing right there in her robe.

"Lin... middle of the movie... he's never here, never here when needed... middle of the movie... all I get... " The click told me she was off the line.

Madame Bovary disappeared and I was left in the booth shaking, holding my breath instead of furious. My stomach heaved. I made it to my bed, dizzy and light headed. I couldn't tell anyone. Instead, I was relieved to be distracted by the hive of activity, a dormitory filled with strangers who were becoming my friends. In the dining hall, at the café, in the dressing room of the dance studio—we circled each other with tentative offerings of friendship. WASP preppies held back and let us city girls know the gulf was too wide. We couldn't make it across the divide of privilege. Even the well-to-do city girls didn't try, not until later in the college years when these distinctions had been blurred by remarkableness, talent, or sheer proximity. Abundant plumbing (bathrooms connecting bedrooms) made for luxurious shared living, encouraging unlikely and sometimes life-long connections.

The next note pinned to my door would change everything for me, for the three of us. It was the one that said to call Flower Fifth Avenue Hospital, where my mother had undergone an emergency hysterectomy. Knowing nothing about the effects of this surgery, I considered the possibility that this was another of my mother's stunts, the ultimate interruption. But I took the train to Grand Central and then the bus instead of a cab to the hospital. I was in no hurry.

Sitting behind a large black woman with a small girl at her side, I was soothed by her Jamaican accent which reminded me of Levita padding around the apartment picking up after us and ever so slowly bringing tea to my mother. The woman leaned down to her daughter and murmured, "You know, you're not a tiny girl anymore ... you're a big girl now." Her large arm encircled the child as if to tell her she was still beloved, still protected even as she was growing up.

"No, no ... I's just a tiny baby, a tiny baby ... up in de arm!" The child sang out loudly, turning some of the heads on the bus. And then, pleased with her discovery kept going, "Up in de arm, up in de arm," she chanted, her tiny fingers playing on her mother's sleeve.

My father was waiting in the hospital corridor, in front of the closed door.

"A grapefruit, they found a tumor the size of a grapefruit." He gave me a quick hug and kept talking: "It's been rough." He didn't look at me, didn't use my mother's name. Whatever she'd endured wasn't part of his picture. He too, must have assumed that this emergency surgery was just another episode in the string of outbursts, her mid-forties outbursts that no one was connecting with menopause.

"Go in. I'll wait here." He nearly shoved me towards the closed door.

"Mom?" Her eyes were closed like those times when Levita guided me towards her bed, helping me to be the right daughter. And now as then, my heart pounded when I was close enough to touch her.

"You made it." She opened her eyes but turned away, pulling the tubes across her exposed shoulder.

"I knew you would," she said into the pillow.

I was tempted to straighten the tubes, to keep fluids going to the right places, but I didn't reach out for fear of touching her bare skin. Since seventh grade, I'd stood back, no longer expecting a hug, a real kiss on my cheek. She'd offer her cheek, averting her eyes. Her skin, like her touch, was unfamiliar except for those times when she ripped off her blouse or came out of the bedroom in her slip, muttering angrily, both exposed and hidden—a mystery.

I was ashamed at how calm I felt seeing the tubes festooned across her, imagining the deep wound hidden beneath the sheets. I stood beside the bed for a few more moments, not taking in the painful surgical event, but how the operation had stopped her in her tracks. Tied up in a bed, her kinetic force stilled. I was in a room with my mother who had big cuts, who was momentarily quiet, and who seemed more manageable than she'd been in a long time.

After the surgery and with no estrogen to support her instant menopause, scenes became much more than temper tantrums. *Uncontrollable* was what my father said when he made the appointment with the mild-mannered psycho-therapist who happened to have an office a block from our apartment on West End Avenue but was totally incapable of making a diagnosis, which might have led to medication. The three of us met with the aloof pipe smoker once or twice for consultation, for "family guidance" which was, in fact, family non-guidance.

As my mother moved from the sofa to the chair, from the window to the bookcases, her mouth never stopped. I'd come to think of her as a mouth.

"Never there when needed... I sailed on *The Liberté*... I try, goddamn it I try... you two! You think I don't know... my undarling daughter!"

All Dr. Podel offered this wild manic woman was *talk,* when it was clear that she needed to be contained, her brain slowed down with whatever would get her to stop! I longed to bring him to our apartment on one of the wild nights of non-stop ravings down the long hallway, to see my mother in action, in her natural habitat. Instead, he sat behind his desk, making notes on a yellow pad, as if the pad would reveal a course of action.

The three of us left his office that evening with my mother still talking, hurling accusations. We were on West End Avenue with folks coming home from work, carrying briefcases, groceries, flowers.

"Sons of bitches!" She cuts in front of my father.

"Bea, we're almost home. I'll start dinner."

Does he think a promise of supper will divert the manic river of words that's been raging for days and nights? We didn't have more than a block to go to get back to our apartment. How could the doctor have sent us back alone with her? Why didn't he follow us to the eighth floor and see for himself?

I wanted her to be both seen and hidden, wanted a witness and yet was queasy at the possibility of exposing her, my crazy mother. I didn't take comfort from looking more like Ted's daughter than Bea's. I didn't know if my father was helpless and couldn't protect me or if he was finished with her—and even with me?

As my freshman year progressed, my father was undone by the outbursts and probably more terrified than he was admitting. He lured me home on weekends with tickets to plays, the ballet, and even more seductively, with the admission that he missed me. The ambulance rides began that year.

"You have to come home!" My father's voice had been hoarse, the way it was when things were really bad. "I'm worn out. State law says someone has to accompany a patient to a mental hospital. She can't be alone in the ambulance." "I've got my first mid-term paper due tomorrow," I whispered into the dorm phone.

Sarah Lawrence was a short train ride from Grand Central. I caved in and arrived as the ambulance was pulling up in front of our building. My father gave me a quick hug and ushered me into the ambulance. I will be the one on the jump seat. Although unable to claw my wrist, my mother still had her most lethal weapon. She tried to bellow, as she had in scenes at home but the straitjacket made it impossible. Instead, I heard a croaking, a gasping: "Teddy's little girl! Bitch! Selling me out! We're not such good friends!" And then in a whisper, "You're my lifeline." The driver caught my eye in the mirror and smiled sheepishly, almost in apology for being a witness. When he checked his side-view mirror, he didn't see my hand on hers, now that it was safe to touch her. Did I reach to comfort her? Or to reassure myself that I was braver than I felt? I knew what she was in for in 1956. The straitjacket would be removed only after sedation, when the tongue depressor was in place and electroshock treatment had begun. Her mania machine would be stopped, the psychosis in retreat. For a few weeks, she will seem becalmed—before catatonia returned and the cycle resumed.

She closed her eyes, and for an instant I imagined she just needed to rest. Her sweat streaked cheeks glistened in the dim light. Half of me was in sheer terror at the specter of my trussed mother; the other half was relieved that for a while, she was someone else's problem. I was too young, at eighteen, to know that when people make you worry, and create pulsing fear, they also make you furious.

My first semester was punctuated with her unraveling. As hard as I tried to disappear into books and ideas, offering the wider world, my father kept pulling me back to the explosions on West 83rd Street. A few weeks before my graduation, he will leave her, and I will become her primary, if not legal, custodian—the manager of the unmanageable.

I couldn't resist his requests especially when I knew him to be a man of few words, this father who seemed more reliable than the raging mother. He was, after all, not the crazy parent. He had made it clear that if not for me he'd have left her, would have disappeared into the park foliage beyond the bay window of the new apartment on

Central Park West. In the same way that some parents redecorate their children's rooms just before they depart for college, my parents had moved to our largest apartment the summer before my freshman year.

"Finally," my father exclaimed to my mother, "you've arrived on Central Park West!" There was the usual mixture of pride and derision he gave to the things he could pay for, at the loss of the artist's life he'd planned.

After years of eating in the living room, we now had a formal dining room with a faux Sheridan mahogany set of matching tables, chairs and a sideboard that held a pair of silver candlesticks nervously chosen by my mother. She had some innate good taste but was cowed when faced with putting it all together, as if sets or matching pairs flew in the face of her random, patched together self.

The dining room must have given her a new cue: suddenly butter pats imprinted with a clover leaf arrived on a Dresden plate from her kitchen which still had the makings of test tube discoveries—uptown or downtown, our kitchens remained the same. These butter pats were a random gesture like the unmatched white gloves that, as a little girl, I had lined up in her bureau drawer.

The phrases I'd heard as a kid remained part of her repertoire on Central Park West—mad money, putting on my face, rolling with the punches—by now, were out of context and the rush of words, an encoded language, was bewildering. Gone was the Mom who with the tilt of her hat, a tug on its veil and a spritz of cologne seemed buoyed, even confident. The sudden appearance of her shoulders or her breasts freed from the binding brassiere ("It's cutting me in two!" she'd shriek) could never be connected with her hand on my back singing me to sleep on 10ᵗʰ Street. I didn't *decide* that it hurt less to forget the soft mother than to feel the loss. Incrementally the original film just faded and I was in another movie. I couldn't know then that the soft mother would only be retrieved when she was dead or as she said about the dead, *gone*, mysteriously disappeared.

Freshman year I was breathlessly leapfrogging away from home—to my books, to new friends. As I was revealing myself, inch by inch, to my boyfriends, I also imagined my mother half-naked in the faux mahogany dining room tearing at her blouse while my father ate hurriedly, his face bowed to his plate. This didn't occur simultaneously, but it happened in a kind of ambush. Without warning, images over lapped, intersected. The middle of her movie became the middle of my movie.

Whenever I mentioned my parents, I left out the details, protecting her, protecting me. To tell and not to tell was a real dilemma, as real as my dry mouth, my queasy stomach. These signals were becoming more powerful than any words; I was discovering the language of symptom, the powerful *false figures* the Gestalt analysts identify as stand-ins for the real problem: perfect distractions.

My mother's first commitment to a mental hospital came a few months after her hysterectomy. Blazing color was at its height, and I was deep into choices: ideas which will become term papers, friendships which will last a lifetime; deciding each morning who to be that day, and heading the list, which boy would be the candidate for my eventual deflowering.

This time there was no note. I was called to the phone booth in the corridor.

"Linda dear," my father's voice was confidential, important. "Your mother's in a mental hospital."

I heard *your mother*. She was my mother, my problem. My eighteen-year-old-self stiffened. I'd taken care of her since I could walk but now it was official. Flooded with adrenaline, I pleaded silently, don't *make me take this on alone.*

Somehow my father had gotten her into the car and driven to The Pinewood Sanatorium in Westchester, committing her against her will. In those days men could put their crazy wives in sanitariums and drive home along the Saw Mill Parkway with more relief than they'd felt in years. It was ten years before lithium and other pharmacological cocktails will give manic depressives and their families a break.

A week later, we found Bea sitting on the sun porch, staring blankly at the burnished yellow leaves. In a move to get her to respond, I sat closer to her, the way I did when I was small, when she smoked and read.

"Mom, can you hear me? I want you to . . . " My tone was firm, to put myself in the driver's seat, to have the illusion of power when I was close to blacking out for the first time in my life, like migraine sufferers who describe the *aura* that signals the headache. Her nearly frozen stare, her stillness gave me the creeps. This was new, this catatonic Mother. There was no response, not even to the pressure of my shoulder against her shoulder in the hospital gown. Her hazel eyes were more opaque than usual, their light brown clouded, unfocused.

I turned to my father who stood behind us in the doorway. His eyes were on the horizon, as if there could be horizon in the airless room. With my free hand, knowing he wanted to be out of that sunroom, out of our lives, I gestured for him to leave us alone.

"What did they do? " I put my arm around her shoulder as if we're old friends.

She stared straight ahead as if talking to herself: "When I went to breakfast and there was nothing at my place, I knew it was D Day and I would be taken down again... to that yellow house, the little one... where they do the shock... strapped my arms...." She stretched her arms out, to show the marks which so horrify me that I'll wipe them out so they will remain *indescribable* even for a describer, although the bars on her windows will always return and will years later keep me from visiting animal shelters, finding my rescues in the street.

She won't be saying more about the treatment because electroshock therapy wipes out memory and will keep some of it wiped, forever. Her voice was raspy, as if the power was interrupted, like static on the radio. (Thorazine had given her permanent static.) She gazed at the trees and lengthening shadows and suddenly jumped back to being ten, coming home from a country outing with *her* mother who was usually too overwhelmed, with a household of six children, to take her anywhere. The static was replaced with an almost lilting cadence as if she were reciting a favorite poem, "... wrapped in wildflowers ... Black Eyed Susans." Her face softened. Was it comforting to leave the treatment story and go back into the wildflowers? For once, not finishing a story was a blessing and not just her trademark.

As we sat in the fading light, I longed for that Black Eyed Susan girl to have become my mother instead of this one, sitting silently in this place where others are even crazier than she is. There was pressure in my throat, as if I should be saying something, doing something to *undo* what's happened. But I just stroked her cold hand, lying immobile in her lap. She was a marionette whose strings had been let down, leaving her crumpled, and her face a mask. No restraints were needed now. If only they *were* needed it would be a sign of life in my limp mother, who was no longer spewing words but reaching for them, one by one.

When the aide appeared to lead her away, my arms didn't work. For a moment, I couldn't move... then stood to hug her. She was so small, without the British Brevits, without the tweeds. I put my arms around the crisp cotton gown and held her for an instant, before she pulled away.

"We're not such good friends, anyway . . . ." she muttered as she was led out by the stony attendant.

My father and I sped away with the top down, heading for an early supper at a restaurant. His mouth was set. I knew better than to tell him how I felt. I couldn't risk his anger or even his half-hearted response. He was the normal parent driving me down the highway, on a golden fall day.

As we passed through the village of Katonah, I spotted a flower shop. Without a word, he handed me money. The saleswoman didn't look up when I told her the bouquet was to be delivered to Pinewood.

She carefully spelled my mother's name and took the bills. Those resplendent, buttery roses proclaimed my life-long desire to make nice, to tidy up my mother's room, her kitchen, her slipshod diagnosis, to arrange bouquets, as if her fate could be repaired with purposeful composition, a still-life instead of a swirling mess.

I could be mesmerized by the image of the electroshock literally jolting the juices out of her, as she lay unconscious on the table, removing her will, winding her down. Some of these images flooded me on the rides back with my father or even more vividly when I lay on my bed in the dorm, holding my arms at my side, imagining the straps digging into her skin, my skin.

It will be years before I try to piece together (without success) the whole of her—the woman who tore at her blouses, hurled crayons at me, and left casseroles to mold in the fridge, or the woman whose smile could draw me close even if her eyes never met mine. And even more years to admit how much I missed the mother who sat beside me at Loew's Sheridan—the spunky, not-crazy Mom of my Village days—as we both bathed in the magic of Technicolor, and Betty Grable's flashing smile.

There will be many visits to Pinewood in those college years. Back and forth Bea will go, from the city to what she calls "the country," as if the psychiatric hospital was a picnic spot. Without adequate medication and still suffering from the effects of shock therapy, she will return to Central Park West and to life with a man who was planning his escape but still buying her expensive fur coats.

I sympathized with his confusion because I remembered listening for his key in the lock when I was small, longing for his return—to light up the gloomy apartment with his pleasure in me and his I Can Sell You The Brooklyn Bridge smile.

14

B y the middle of freshman year, a political science trip to McGill introduced me to a large university teeming with a variety of students and to a tall, ruddy cheeked sophomore who wore three piece suits, and walked like Prince Philip with his hands clasped behind his back. Collin was features editor of *The McGill Daily* and the official greeter for our little band from Sarah Lawrence. Within minutes of arriving at the *Daily* office, I was beguiled by this young man, who led me purposefully away from the others and began his playful interrogation,

"So. New York. So. Sarah Lawrence. What brings you to our frozen parts?"

His all-out pleasure in his own delivery, his infectious smile, the rolled up shirt sleeves and the pin striped flannels, the studied nonchalance with which he carried his large frame all created the impression that just getting up in the morning was a good thing if you were Collin W. Geisman.

Later that evening, standing at the foot of the Victorian staircase at our small hotel, his face flushed, his dark hair glistening from the light snow that'd begun to fall, he studied me as I descended. We were both intent on making too much of the moment, on having a marvelous time with a stranger.

I was filled with a kind of daring I'd not felt on home ground. The stage was set for a romance that will always have *distance* as its major description. With my Monday morning departure looming, we behaved like a war time couple, as if we'd been raised on the same movies.

Collin's parka had a deep hood, which created a little tent as he bent towards me. Staring into each other's eyes, encased in layers of wool, we kissed and kissed in the park near the hotel. Movie-style kissing, I'd never known before, in a cold stillness. I ran headlong into a world of Russian steppes and furtive embrace. Gone, in one night, was my obsession with Madame Bovary and in her place, the Russian heroines. Collin would remain as uninformed about these transports as about the dramas at home on Central Park West. Mystery would serve Romance, and mystery would keep the secret of my mother.

A girls' school and a boyfriend hundreds of miles away is ideal for fantasizing about boys, who are most intriguing when absent, being *recalled.* Late night debates with my roommate Franny, revolved around Collin. Now, also gone, were speculations on the Bloomsbury Group or Freudian theory. It was as if all these ideas had been a diversion, a foil for my real work, the *beat beat beating* of my heart.

Or as Marcy will say years later, we were most of all driven by Eros. Not the history of civilization. Being the first young woman on my mother's side to go to college didn't occur to me as I flirted with ideas and the young Canadian, who wanted me to meet his parents on my second visit. I didn't know if this was a sign of anything more than his living at home, like so many other students at McGill.

Walking between walls of hard packed snow that seemed to be permanent structures, Collin held my elbow, guiding me ever so carefully towards their Westmont house. I liked being held in the grip of someone trustworthy. I'd read and reread Joyce's *The Dead* and now embraced snow as metaphor. I was perfecting *narrative* as a means to frame whatever could be too intense, to make me an observer instead of, God forbid, someone overwhelmed. Standing in the doorway had served me as a child.

The Victorian house with its cement lions guarding the front steps rose out of the whiteness, in a blush of pale sandstone. Inside was gleaming solid mahogany, not the veneer of our dining room table, and damask silk wallpaper in a second sitting room. Even my fanciest West Side friends had only one living room.

At dinner, Collin's parents sat at either end of the table as we took our places in the middle. The chandelier cast an overly bright light on the four of us, suggesting that we could as well be having an appendectomy. At seven in the evening, his father was as impeccable as he must have been at nine in the morning. Without a trace of shadow on his cheek, Mr. Geisman adjusted his French cuffs and buttered his roll with the deliberation I imagined accompanied all his gestures, even as a businessman. He was mostly silent but listened attentively when I spoke and smiled when I finished. A French maid passed the platters with silver tongs while Mrs. Geisman, a professor of medieval literature, whose sallow complexion was made more so with too much powder, questioned me about my studies. I didn't flinch because I was confident in my opinions, buoyed by weekly conferences with my professors. Queries about my parents, however, made me long for another one on Chaucer.

"Advertising, is it? Is that your father's work?" Her gray eyes were steady, not unlike the passport control officer who had hours before admitted me to Canada. Whether for tact or disinterest, Mrs. Geisman didn't probe when I said my mother didn't work. I left out her painting because in those days I couldn't describe my mother as anything but crazy. It will be years before I can admit she's an artist and even more before I hang her work. I couldn't give my mother a seat at the Geismans' table.

Collin cut his meat with exquisite concentration and suddenly diverted her,

"At Sarah Lawrence there's a don system, Mother, just like at Oxford." He studied her face. And when she nodded, he turned back to the perfectly roasted lamb which, in that instant, brought back my frantic mother with her charred roast and my father's scowl. But with the same speed I was back, pirouetting, showing off, waltzing at their cotillion. The young man opposite me was their prince: tall and dark-haired like his father, with the piercing eyes of his mother. Mr. Geisman was recessive, the father as prop, whereas Mrs. Geisman shared the spotlight with her intense son, whose cheeks were flushed with excitement, as he commanded the stage at our table.

Thankfully, Collin's confident good humor saved him from being the stuffed shirt his mother was priming for the Rhodes scholarship which will take him to Oxford.

My first months at Sarah Lawrence had prepared me for the Geismans. We met with our professors weekly, honing our skills as academic concubines when they were male and worshipful devotees when they were female.

Tonight we all sat beneath the warm light, our faces slightly flushed (except for Claire Geisman's which remained powder dry) doing our best for the eager young man we all loved. Compelled to impress his parents I became the interviewee,

"My favorite course right now is Art and Visual Perception, with Rudolph Arnheim. It's so wonderful to work with him." Their non-reaction told me that Arnheim meant nothing to them.

When dinner was over, Mr. and Mrs. Geisman retired to their sitting room, not the main living room, and Collin and I went upstairs to the library. I'd never seen so many possibilities for privacy, although we would not, as it turned out, know what to do with ours. The Geismans must have trusted their boy to keep to the rules of Westmont, which meant never entering your sweetheart, just lying on the leather sofa, holding tightly until you both might suffocate, lambs wool upon lambs wool, never skin meeting skin.

When I could no longer bear the suspense, I would say good-night and go to the surgically white tiled bathroom and lie in the deep tub, dreamily swirling suds around my eighteen-year-old body. I was still the same, still a virgin, quivering from the embracing, the yearning, disappointed in a terse, unnamed way. *Momentous* was what I also felt as I lay there in the warm suds, imagining more of Collin but holding back, to match his holding. I assumed, at a moment of his choosing, Collin W. Geisman would relieve me of my burdensome virginity.

After my bath, I went to the guest room, just a wall away from Collin's, where his trophies punctuated the bookshelves. His triumphs were there, even if he wasn't. Nearly lightheaded from the hot bath, I got into the perfectly made bed. The maid, who'd skewered the lamb, had made the bed with lavender scented sheets. Had Claire Geisman provided sachets for the closets, or had the French woman seen to that? I was captivated by every detail, drawn into a family who would never welcome my parents even if Sarah Lawrence distinguished me, like having perfect teeth.

I never brought up the Little Red School House or my Village years. I was happy to be *incognito* and to leave my mother behind, really behind now as I was practically in the Tundra. For weekends in Montreal, black stockings and long skirts were retired, and instead woolen dresses in soft pastels were carefully chosen, my long dark hair twisted and pinned up. As a New Yorker (who had no information about being Jewish) and with a purposeful mid-Atlantic accent, could I nearly have been the British prize the Geismans dreamed for their son?

Collin and I were right for each other's timidity, until the summer of my sophomore year when I agreed to be a counselor at a Jewish summer camp, in order to be near Montreal, near Collin, who was to be an intern at *The Montreal Star*. By this time we'd rubbed and rubbed, our lips bruised from hours of kissing, and were on the way to more formal ties, perhaps an engagement.

As I was packing for my Canadian summer, Collin called to say, without a trace of chagrin, that he was being "lured away" by a Yugoslavian scholarship. A tempting excursion into the "Eastern Riviera" as it was called. At first, it seemed peculiar that he'd take this prize when I was coming to the Laurentians, for him, for our chance to finally sleep together. But I absorbed the blow of his double-cross seamlessly. I was in the business of making nice, not causing the kind of trouble I knew from home. Instead of showing how hurt I was, I behaved like a junior version of Mrs. Geisman, urging him to take the scholarship, another prize for his trophy shelf.

Collin and I were always at the movies.

15

Pripstein's summer camp was the closest I would ever come to a kibbutz. Ardent young men from Eastern European immigrant families encircled the campfire, like graceful or not so graceful hunters. These were not Collin or the familiar Central Park West specimens, the easily dissuaded collegiate swains I had known up to then. These young McGill men wanted action, completion, not postponement.

As soon as I'd unpacked my trunk and told my charges, my eleven-year-old girls, to pipe down, I joined the circle around the fire, riveted by the confident McGill boys who returned summer after summer to make love in every nook and cranny of Pripstein's.

Before I had received Collin's first postcard from the Dalmatian coast I'd caught the attention of two Montrealers: Henry and Leonard. Henry, the son of a Ukrainian greengrocer, was a political scientist with a formidable academic future. Leonard's first book of poetry *Let Us Compare Mythologies* was the first book published by the McGill Poetry Series in 1956, just months before the Pripstein's summer. It will be eight years before Leonard Cohen will be catapulted to fame, after Judy Collins will bring him on stage to sing "Suzanne" for the first time before an audience.

There was no time to miss Collin or to find his postcards too collegiate, less than claiming. I bade goodbye, goodbye to his stone lions, to being inspected through his parent's lorgnettes, and to the rubbing that left us fretful, always on the verge, never in afterglow, always tantalized.

Henry and Leonard presented alternatives to my Westmont prize, the college boy who dared not dare but clutched and released me simultaneously. Before I could memorize the daily schedule and get my girls to activities on time, I realized I'd become the exotic, unfamiliar New York girl who by very definition of not being from *there,* was *someone.* My high school days of running breathlessly to *The Liberte´* for a glimpse of Paul Vallé, had set me in pursuit of the *other,* but it had not occurred to me until Collin, that I too, could be the foreigner.

Saying as little about my parents as possible put me one step from orphan-hood. I never outright lied about home or my parents, who still occupied 4B on Central Park West. I left out the details, not knowing that when you need to disown your mother, you've thrown out the model and are flying without a net as a young woman, the cost of which will be deferred, haunting you for decades.

After a day in the sun which left its scent on our skin, counselors sat around the campfire, our eyes shining like those of the raccoons who circled the bunks after dark. There were midnight skinny dips with lake water as heavy as velvet rippling across my nipples. If I could have seen the guy's rumps and penises clearly, I would have stayed on shore or not come down to the lake at all. It was the cloak of inky night that made me freer than I really was. On so-called *wilderness* campouts we tied knots, laid down tarps, and paid rapt attention to one another and not to our kiddies.

I had left my mother to my father that summer and felt safer at Pripstein's than at the college. The only phone was in the office, which must have restrained my mother as Mr. and Mrs. Pripstein manned the office and took calls in their heavily accented Polish English. There was no fooling around with the Pripsteins. Leaving a message wasn't encouraged, so it was up to me to make my weekly call. Inexplicably my mother accepted the length and breadth of the call. There were no attacks, and I could be back in the sunshine without needing time to compose myself, to arrange my face.

After our kids were in for the night, we sat around the fire, listening to Leonard and his guitar:

"Blue lakes and blue skies, pine trees climbing high... .all our friends are nigh."

His eyes half-closed, his head thrown back, his nasal call invited us to witness his communion with the night sky. All the young women were invited, whether or not they had boyfriends. Mine was far across the world, choosing another scholarship prize instead of me.

I was torn between the poet who was a collector and the political scientist who was a tender appreciator. Both young men had eclipsed Collin and both, unknowingly, presented life choices. While I trailed after enigmatic Leonard, awaiting a nod or even a shrug of interest, Henry dubbed me the Trauma counselor even before I took over the theater club. Beguiled but not blind to my wiring, Henry could have grounded me—if I'd been aware of my addiction to chaos and dared to give it up, dared to be anchored, even protected. For even here, in the middle of the mountains, far from my mother's troubles, the films of Pinewood still ambushed me. I'd see her room with its barred window, her sightless vacant stare as I entered the visitor's lounge, her movements stiffened from the shock treatments... my mother and me, no longer pals at Loew's Sheridan, but still, despite my efforts at distance, so joined that her hysteria was mine and her electroshocked eyes also mine.

I couldn't separate from her—my attacking, seductive mother, even while safe in this Canadian kibbutz. The waste, the irony of it was she never knew I was so entangled as she heaved and sighed or was silent, a small lone figure in the hospital sunroom. My allegiance was lost on her. When I'd offered a goodbye kiss, she would hiss. I was rushing the visit like my father, the enemy. All in all I was totally useless she'd mumble, as she grabbed my wrist, her nails cutting in.

The last time she'd paused in her farewell attack, suddenly smiling her beautiful closed mouth smile of my childhood, I caved in not just because of the smile but because an hour before, in one of her ramblings, she'd told me how her own raging mother had bitten *her* shoulder when she was four. This mother she would carelessly harm, ten years later, when Sophie lay dying from diabetes and fifteen-year-old Bea accidentally emptied the bed pan, pouring out the urine needed for testing. Still not looking at me, she described her mother's screams as the catheter was reinserted. This unknown grandma was the one in the mutton-sleeve blouse I could barely make out in the album. The one wrapped in wildflowers?

Determined to be lost in poetry, instead of found by the decent social scientist, I accepted Leonard's surprising weekend invitation to his studio in Montreal's French quarter. As the somber young man slowly swept aside the velvet curtain, I was admitted to his Kasbah.

Even as the sun blazed on St. Helena Street, it was Eternal Evening in those shadowed, nocturnal rooms.

Ruby and burnt orange were the colors I will take from that weekend, low-wattage light bulbs and the round-shouldered outline of the poet as he brewed tea, sighed and never made a move towards me. Relieved and intrigued, I lay curled on Leonard's velvet throw, my head cradled by the embroidered pillows, under a spell of words. His mournful, insistent, nasal voice (which would become his signature) was the stroke, the embrace I wasn't sure I wanted. Instead, I was relieved to be introduced to the Mysterious, to Stillness as power, as he declared he was born out of a long dedicated lineage.

"You can invent a magical family," he promised, sprinkling his litany with quotes from the Baal Shem Tov: "It is because things happen once that the individual partakes of Eternity . . ." and between sips of lukewarm tea intoned, "the greatest Evil is when you forget that you are the son of a King."

Irresistible! To be other than the child of one's parents! As I sank deeper into the brocade pillows, Leonard crooned,

"Be one of the dancing, deep-skinned people . . . they are the ones who know the sun, who hear music others will never hear."

As if this were not enough to mess me up, to throw me off the Collin or Henry track, he then whispered, "The women I love are as beautiful as gypsies . . ."

Returning to Pripstein's that Sunday evening, having given only my mind (a distinction the world will learn later from "Suzanne"), I'd been converted and with "seeker," "scrutiny," had a new vocabulary with which to bedevil myself and others. Visions of Hasidic dancers had been offered up to the Greenwich Village girl—who couldn't know she'd been set upon a course that will marry her to Yeats, keeping her from the good boys, drawn to the bad boys.

When I learned Leonard's mother had also spent time in a sanatorium, I wondered what the cost had been to him.

Despite my infatuation with infatuation, Collin and I resumed when he returned. Still the good listener, I paid attention to tales of hitchhiking through Yugoslavia, surviving on bread and sardines and tomatoes. Maybe I thought that he'd be bolder, as if the sardine detail was the omen I was watching for, but sophomore year brought more sexual minuets, and by spring we probably both hoped a month at Harvard summer school would break our record of abstinence.

The closest we came was lying naked in candlelight in the Harvard Square apartment I shared with a Sarah Lawrence friend—staring solemnly, so locked on each other's eyes that I doubt we took in our bodies. Gone were the wool sweaters we'd rubbed against, but both of us were still timid, and the sparsely furnished room was too crowded with our parents who might as well have been encircling us in the shadows... his mother brandishing the pointer she used on the blackboard, my mother tearing at her blouse (to distract), and our fathers turning their backs, their hands over their ears.

When Collin left for Oxford the fall of my junior year, with the Rhodes scholarship his mother had been plotting since his birth, I was both let down and relieved, filled with ambivalence that was to become my most constant companion.

Our implied contract had been torn. Collin's urging me on to graduate school in Wales was vetoed by my Dad, who couldn't be behind a plan that would keep me a student and hold me back from earning. A Master's in Middle English! What was I thinking?

My father's once vibrant voice was now nearly a whisper, as he reported from the front. His asthma was worse, and he blamed the breathless attacks on Buffy, who was somehow surviving my absence, fed by my father, but walked during the day by my wild mother who could just as well let go of his leash on Central Park West. I didn't see then that our feisty blond dog was being set up as the cause of the trouble between them. My mother was off on a tangent, sprinkling her ravings with references to Buffy as the respiratory irritant that was sending my father into the night on longer and longer walks. I was half listening, determined to shut her out long enough to propel myself into my own drama. Before I could move into my Next Chapter (I was supported by titles as if they were life rafts), there was the matter of losing the albatross of my virginity. If Collin was not going to be the one, I was determined to find a substitute.

After junior year, in early summer, working at my father's office, I found my candidate. Tom was perfect, a playwright with a kind of literary nonchalance, able to give the nod to the moment without giving anything, other than his writing, much importance. The contrast to Leonard was striking.Writing was still what mattered, but Tom left out the incantations, the smoke and mirrors.

If you were up for some playful verbal tennis matches and off-hand hugs as he drew you against his side, checking his messages, or returning a phone call, Tom was the one. He even kissed absentmindedly.Ten years older and deep into a career that would, a few years later, take him to Broadway, his passion for the theater came first. He would be the first to instill the misconception that lying down with writers would make me one too.

Tom was attractive in an unintended way, with Midwestern easy looks that belied his Eastern European parents, an Experienced Man of the Stage, and an amputee due to a childhood accident. The leg detail was not a detail at all. I was already captivated by the irregular and abnormal, primed for rescuing someone. Tom's loss made him irresistible. His missing lower leg was a character in the little play he was creating with me, over a few meetings. They couldn't be called dates, more like pretexts for coming over to his place. One of those evenings, with the city sounds coming in with the humid summer breeze, I lay beneath him and realized that it was his absent leg seducing me. Without the romantic minuet, the candlelight staring contest I had with Collin, I was being carried along by Tom's affliction. As if he were reading Braille, he closed his eyes and stroked my breast.

"I'm not sure ... let's wait ..." My arm covered my face.

He stopped and gently took my arm down. He was smiling in his off-hand way and whispered, "Don't ... don't make such a big deal of this." There was enough authority in the voice, in the sureness of his hand, that I was relieved of the big deal.

I lay still and let him in. Without the usual drama of desire and denial, there was no rush at all. I was sore and surprised by how scraped I felt. Tom's complete collapse onto my steamy breasts was alarming. Had he fainted? Was this what happened to them? I waited for him to move off me. I also waited for him to speak. He fell back into the sheets, his stump of a thigh still covered and his penis flaccid against the harness which kept his wooden leg attached. I wondered if he ever made love wholly unclothed with everything in plain sight.

As he dozed, I dressed quickly and left. There was no regret, just let there be a taxi! When I got home, I was so unsure of what happened that I had to check under the hot shower to see if there was any blood. There was enough to assure me that the Rubicon had been crossed. My collegiate obsession was over. My parent's uninterrupted sleep was a bonus as I slipped into my room and sank into my childhood bed, with Buffy curled behind my knees, to replay the moment, to examine it for more than I'd actually felt.

In the fall, I was welcomed back as an anointed bride, not given to anyone but seen with new eyes. A few dorm mates sat cross-legged on the carpet in my room, leaning forward, to learn more. "So, come on . . . how was it? An older guy . . . he must have been great." My opera-loving friend, Fay, squinted into the lamplight as if she were conjuring up the scene, the way she listened to *La Bohème,* snug in the corner of her bed.

"A night worth waiting for," I said, "he was wonderful . . . I was so nervous but he was so sweet."

And then firmly, "It makes a big difference with someone experienced."

The pill had not yet appeared, and diaphragms were the newest accessory. My friends directed me to Park Avenue, always a suspect street for a Village girl, where an overbearing German Jewish gynecologist led the charge against pure pleasure. With a crooked finger and a heavy accent, she warned of accidents and described the slippery diaphragm as if it had a life of its own, ready to elude my best intentions.

16

In the late Fifties, Sarah Lawrence was a place where every adventure, whether with ideas or with men was given equal time. There was endless debate about allowing men to dominate our lives. Unleashed from matronly mothers, who visited in suits and sensible shoes, some of us modeled ourselves after Isadora Duncan, with flowing hair and dramatic gestures. Having graduated from Madame Bovary and the Russian steppes, I was awash with Colette and committed to memory the moment in *The Vagabond* when the narrator dismisses her lover, "I refuse to see all the beautiful countries of the world reflected in the amorous mirror of your eyes." And with that, she's off to join the circus.

Now I had an image to put between me and my worries. My father was warning that no man would marry me if he knew about my mother. Was it my seed they would fear, could I pass this craziness on, or was I already a pale negative others could see developing as I aged? I vowed to be a vagabond who wouldn't need the protection my father was warning I might not have anyway. I would wear black stockings for more years than any of my friends.

In August, before my senior year, my newly minted ideal of independence would be tested. Without warning I needed surgery for an anal ulcer. Coming out of the anesthesia, I cried out for my mother who was locked up in Pinewood. The more I sobbed the more I felt burning spasms in the anal wound, a nerve center. A psychiatrist was summoned and declared I was hysterical but not psychotic, whereupon my father bolted for the cafeteria. He returned with a malted and after depositing it on my nightstand, fled again. If he didn't flee, it's still how I see him leaving the room.

Having avoided the psych ward, I went back to our apartment. That afternoon, as I lay in bed without Buffy, who had to stay on the floor because of the operation, my Sarah Lawrence friend Gail appeared with ramekins of baked custard, fragrant with vanilla. Something a mother would make.

In those sultry summer weeks after the operation, and before classes started, my father came home early from work and cooked our dinners or brought in Broadway delicacies... a buttery slice of smoked salmon, rotisserie chicken still warm in the bag, a Napoleon to remind me of the ones I'd loved in the Village. He brought the food on a tray and kept me company. I ate propped on an elbow, unable to sit. He didn't ask about the raw wound that had to heal slowly, without stitches. After that first morning in the hospital, when I'd cried out for my mother, I would never again call for her no matter how much I needed her. Correction: I would say her name out loud when I'd fallen into postpartum depression, when I was forced to admit I was still her daughter, somebody's daughter.

The nerve centered pain was the biggest deal I'd ever had in my body. I tried moving without touching off hot stabs, gliding instead of walking. One evening, soaking in the tub, relieved to be finally getting better, I was surprised by the shot of hot pain. My screams brought my father to the edge of the tub. Without a word, he lifted me from the water, and wrapped a towel around me, like when I was three or four and even five. We never mentioned the bathtub event again and never discussed how someone so young could have been growing an ulcer.

Senior year I studied with poets Muriel Rukeyser and Jane Cooper. I read long into the night, transported, despite my mother's alarm bells, which could come as a phone call or a summons from my father. I was so intent on keeping her condition secret that Professor Rudolph Arnheim never knew what had drawn me to my senior project. My paper on "Creativity and Madness" was completed while my mother was in Pinewood a few miles from the college. Compelled and reluctant (always divided), I would ask my father to drive me to the sanatorium.

One afternoon I led my mother outside to a bench in the pale sunlight, the hopeful February light. She wore her usual beret, not tilted jauntily as when she's better, but pulled severely to one side. Her cheeks were sallow and her mouth without lipstick surprisingly small. There'd been another shock treatment a few days before. I took her gloved hand in mine, as if we're meeting for the first time, "It's good to see you, Mom."

She watched a sparrow tweaking the branches of a Chinese witch hazel bush that will bloom early, in March. She turned from the sparrow and looked, for an instant, into my eyes and said, "The top, the top of a baby's head . . . so friendly."

Did she mean me? Am I the baby whose head was friendly? How can the crown of its head be friendly? Is she back in a time when I was friendly, not the enemy like my father? Not the *wrong* baby as she would bellow years later.

The picture of a mysterious baby flooded me with panic, taking over my arms and legs like seeping color. The weakness remained as we walked towards the main building. Cut this out! I wanted to scream, even as I worried that it was my fault that she was the way she was and where she was. This worry had been with me ever since she'd torn open her robe and pointed to the scar on her stomach and screeched into my four-year-old face that she'd been cut for me—when rage had blown her through our apartment, shrieking, "You ripped me open!"

Before I left the lounge, I promised she would be well very soon, in time for my graduation in June. But she was not listening, just standing still, a child waiting for permission. As I moved closer, offering my arm in a half-circle to hold her, she took the arm of the attendant holding her coat. I watched them shuffle down the hall, willing her to turn round, to see me still there.

My father started the car, also without looking at me. It suddenly occurred to me that because my father prefers me, had always preferred me to her—he needs to steer clear of me. It took my breath away to think this as he drove us out of the parking lot. And that moment in Prospect Park, when he'd asked her to have an abortion, is still so fresh for me that it returns in moments like this, when I'm asking "who is this person, and who am I to him?"

We headed back to Manhattan, where I will spend the rest of the weekend with Danny, a West Side boy: handsome, nearly pretty, the son of an Irish Follies girl and a Jewish bootlegger. After his Dad's death, restless and sad, he'd fled Columbia's law school and fell into advertising, a natural for the ad business, moving with grace, wooing the clients. (Danny was a smoothie who would, a few years after I'd rejected his proposal, abandon his new wife and two little baby girls.)

As the elevator, no bigger than a dumbwaiter, deposited me on the landing of his tiny rooftop apartment on West 75th Street, I felt safe. He welcomed me with a light kiss and ran the bath water the way someone else might pour a drink. When he wrapped me in lavender towels, I felt carefully handled, even cherished. Danny was by nature indulgent. Just as he expected the softest cotton against his chest, so he enjoyed giving presents, introducing me to antique garnets when he sent a Victorian broach to our apartment on Valentine's Day. His office messenger had grinned as I signed for the large, lace festooned card. Danny was making money and having fun with it. A regular *bon vivant* my grandmother would have said, with a sigh, if she'd seen the delicacies stashed in his kitchenette: mushrooms marinated in sauces I couldn't pronounce, real caviar, bits of one creature curled within folds of another. In March, bursts of forsythia filled the Chinese jar on his window sill, overlooking the tar papered roof terrace. In that early spring sun, we sat side by side in deck chairs, wrapped in blankets, imagining our trip down the Amazon. With his nearly whispered words, his perfect mambo (we danced wherever we could), and his unhurried touch, I was giving up Colette and giving in to my Central

Park West boy. I suspected he called all his girls "kitten," but for once in my life I let it go. There were no signs of anyone else, and I was finally having a lovely time.

Danny created a bridge from college to the Manhattan world of grown-up jobs and grown-up pleasures. He took me to restaurants I'd never heard of, ordering food I'd only read about, like squid and *tapas* served on ashtray sized plates in gloomy bars. He found tables set up behind grocery stores before Ninth Avenue was the rage and made me feel the amazing crossover from food to sex, and that one led to the other. Before Danny, I was too self-conscious to eat on a date, as if eating was a bodily function to be hidden, a detour from the romantic destination.

Despite the heady, seductive weekends in Manhattan, I wasn't as eager as the other girls to be out of school, to graduate. My mother's psychotic breaks would have finished me if not for my friends and teachers and the credo of the college: take in ideas as if they're meant to be eaten. I wanted to stay where I was.

On Graduation Day, Franny and I were pulling our usual stunt of not being able to leave the campus. At the start of every vacation, we'd always stalled around until the watchman, Ernest, warned he was locking the building and asked why didn't we want to begin vacation anyway? That June morning was our last chance to play the game, to defy the inevitable. Franny's reluctance was mysterious to me, for although her father was controlling in a thunderous way, her stepmother Ruth was irresistible. She made the rambling Flatbush house welcoming. Mexican handicrafts took their place beside

Picasso prints. Every vacation away from Brooklyn was marked with a memento. Ruth murmured, if she joined in at all. If only such a woman could be my step-Mom.

When I had to go back to the Central Park West apartment, which was in shambles, to the wild-eyed woman at the door, I was counting on Buffy to be my comfort, but I also knew he was probably still sniffing out every corner, running from room to room waiting for my father who'd left my mother a few weeks before, after her last return from Pinewood. Had my Dad forgotten I was graduating? Why, I would always want to know, couldn't he have waited a little longer? Danny didn't cushion the day. Away on a business trip, he'd been casual about missing the ceremony and would never know that his absence had marked the beginning of our end, just as I didn't know how quick I was to recoil when protection was denied. I couldn't know then that I was a candidate for phobia—that I was prone to generalizing so that one disappointment would become the title, instead of merely a piece of the story.

Taking my place in the midst of my classmates, I scanned the crowd. My parents would not be coming together, could not even be seated next to one another. Ever since my father had left to live at a midtown hotel, my mother had been in high gear, sleepless and talking to herself and anyone in her vicinity. I knew she was coming with my older cousin, Roy, and that my father was bringing my Grandma Tess, his shield for the afternoon. If he could have held his mother against his chest, he would have. He never looked directly at me anymore, he'd disappeared into a profile.

I adjusted the unbecoming mortar board and took my place in line. Suddenly I spotted my mother darting across the lawn, nearly tripping on the closely arranged rows, waving her program as if she was hailing a cab. To anyone else, she might have seemed excited and heat-struck, but I knew she was searching the crowd for my father. Heat was always one of her many enemies, and today it's creating the combustible figure I spied amidst the well-dressed parents awaiting the stately procession. From my distance, I could only imagine her powdered cheeks streaked with sweat, the red lipstick over her lip line. I knew what color she smeared on her mouth when she was like this, how *tea rose* was forgotten.

She was way ahead of my cousin, moving quickly through the aisles, her hands grasping at the wide-brimmed hat she'd grabbed at the last minute to hide her hair that needs a shampoo. I was too far away to hear her words: all I saw was the steam of her pressing between the chairs, speaking to strangers who looked quickly away holding up their programs, hiding their faces. The silent movie ran for a few minutes with me imagining her crazy talk and then, as suddenly as it erupted, stopped. She took my cousin's arm, like the Queen of England, adjusted the brim of her hat, and sat down.

She hadn't found my father whom I spied in a snappy, beige linen suit, in the very back row with my grandmother who was beaming, proud of her *schöenest kind*. I crossed the stage to accept my diploma, concentrated on not tripping and disowned, once more, the woman fumbling with her purse, crumpling her program.

IV

17

"Everyone leaves home ... Mom ... it's not just me!" Before I could get clear of her, I heard china breaking, and then I was backing up as she hurled another blue and white plate at my head.

"You're killing me!" She screamed, with her hands around my neck, her nails sharp on my throat. Looking up at me, her angry mouth grimacing. Not letting go.

She was shorter than I and unsteady as she flung herself at me. I wanted to shove her to the floor, to slap her down, but instead I pulled her hands down to her sides and held tight to tell her I was stronger. I wanted to hurt her back and was sick with shame for knowing I could.

"Bitch! Bastard! You Sarah Lawrence girl, you." Triumphantly, she'd identified the problem which had become a refrain every time she was this wild. But it's not really our problem. The real problem is that I'm the wrong baby, which I won't hear for another ten years of taking care of her. Not literally in the same household, but keeping her out of mental hospitals, managing the unmanageable.

She swept the unopened mail, coasters and candlesticks to the floor, like someone straightening up. I bolted for my room and locked the door as she pounded, shrieking: "You two! Bastards! Always you two! Teddy's little girl."

Even as my chest heaved, I was safe because the door didn't give as she raved behind it. But I couldn't be sure when she started kicking the bottom. Despite the sticky heat, my hands were cold, my head throbbing as I heard her slam her own door across the hall. It was a relief to hear Buffy's nails on the wood floor as he came out of hiding looking for me. I knew how bad it was when I didn't have the guts to open my own door for my own whimpering dog.

In all the years of bellowing and even biting her own wrists, my mother had never actually hit me any more than she had hugged me. Her blows had always been with words or what she did to herself. The pressure of her hands had been so fast that I couldn't be sure. Had I imagined my neck in her hands? I stood before the mirror looking for signs just as I had after sleeping with David. The faint pink streaks on my throat gave me the real picture, the one I wanted to have *imagined,* because up to that moment, I'd been magically hoping for her blessing, hoping she'd help me move out, move into my new life. As the Rorschach test showed so long ago, Linda doesn't see the whole picture.

I should have known something was coming when she had pushed her favorite dessert away. The heat had built all day. I'd gone out for cold salads from Columbus Avenue in hopes of keeping her out of the kitchen, keeping her calm. But as she'd moved the cutlery, salt shakers, and candlesticks back and forth across the tablecloth, I should have picked up the signs of how manic, how high she was going.

I was so geared up about moving out in the morning that I hadn't connected my move with my father's a few weeks before. Now that he was gone, the apartment felt stripped, my grandmother's Royal

Copenhagen coffee set replaced with unopened mail strewn across the buffet and the walls with telltale marks of his missing watercolors, hanging in his new apartment back in the Village.

After graduating, coming home to his absence was not like coming home at all. I was still so shocked at how abruptly he'd left her and didn't know how long he'd planned his escape that I dodged the subject even if my mother came close to bringing it up. It was easier to let her refer to my father's absence as if it were temporary, like one of his walks in the park with Buffy. She'd been roaming the apartment nightly. When she'd fallen asleep near dawn, I forced myself to get up so that I could have some morning hours of peace, time to pack without the nonstop chatter and time to be alone with Buffy who was standoffish after my four years away. In those early hours I told him how swell he was as I brushed his matted hair that my mother ignored, reminded both of us that I'd be just across the park, not so far, and that I'd be back to see him. I wasn't conscious of leaving him with my mother for company, but it didn't occur to me to take him, either. The kittens Danny had kept, when they were discovered at the college, were now young cats—Sybil (named for my roommate) and Simon.

Buffy wasn't part of my new life, but as he lay between piles of books and clothing, I crooned to him and held his face between my hands. The scent from his long silky ears was close to peanut butter, but his pale blondness and huge brown eyes gave him a nearly human look, like some Hollywood starlet.

As I lay across my bed, still in my clothes, sweat drying on my skin, my Dad's departure came up, as if we two were the *accomplices* she called us. Had his packing made her as crazy as mine did? I could imagine the same flush in her face, the same grimace as she shrieked his name. Had he also been so intent on leaving that he didn't think how terrified she was? Had he stopped to put his arms around her, to tell her he'd be there, if needed? Or had he run, like a thief, through the apartment collecting his things, grabbing his trench coat from the closet the way he did all those times he'd been silent and boiling?

My stomach clenched again. I needed Buffy behind my legs so I could sleep but I was too frightened to unlock the door. I heard him sniffing the floor until he could settle down and sigh in the familiar resigned way that told me he'd be there in the morning.

The next day my mother stood at the front door, barring the moving men from leaving with my bedroom furniture. She was wearing her seersucker summer robe which usually gave her a sunny breakfast look, but now it was afternoon. She hadn't showered and was still in the striped robe.

"Put that back! Take it back!" She shrieked at the burly guys my father had hired to move my things across the park to the East Side.

"Lady, we got no time for this." The larger guy held my dresser, as if it was a book in his hand, and while Buffy danced around his ankles, maneuvered my mother off to the side. Still muttering, she moved obediently, never so crazy to tangle with real authority.

I exited with the furniture and bolted for the staircase. Only two flights kept me from the street, from the cab that will take me across town. As we sped through Central Park's 81st Street transverse, I felt her fingers on my throat. I couldn't know that her imprint will linger and will put my neck off limits forever. If I can make this getaway, I vowed I'll go back to worrying about her, about how she'll manage, for having chased away her few friends, she was now utterly alone with Buffy, who'd given one shrill yelp as I flew past him. I was able to leave my mother's apartment for the Czech-Hungarian mix of the East 70s because my father had agreed to pay my rent until I got my first job. Although he hadn't protected me at graduation, it seemed he didn't want me trapped.

My floor through was just below Gail's. The cold water railroad flats had been converted, with running water and toilets, in the 1920s but the dimly lit, cabbage wafting, halls were straight out of *Crime and Punishment.* Gail had moved in after her mid-term graduation and had already settled into her 5th floor apartment. The 4th floor was mine and painting my kitchen Matisse's brilliant blue was to be my first act of ownership. It was thrilling to be on my own but not really alone.

It was the fall of 1960, and we two post-collegiate girls streamed ahead with our hair flying and our cheeks aflame—unless, like Gail, you were going for the matt porcelain look. My freckles made that impossible, so I blushed my cheeks and paled my mouth, hoping for my own effect. We convinced the phone company that we had a duplex in the old tenement and needed only one line, enabling us to chat for hours curled on our beds a floor apart. The steam pipe running through our apartments was the perfect conduit for our rat-a-tat signals. One tap to chat, two taps for an outside call. Years later when we told stories of this time, our phone maneuver was always at the top of our list of small triumphs: also included were perfecting chocolate mousse and *boeuf bourguignon*, hemming velvet drapes by hand, dragging huge bouquets of Mexican paper flowers home on the crowded rush hour bus, and generally nesting in ways that were intended to make up for having no other place to call home. Gail's had disappeared with the death of her mother, and mine was as off-limits as a condemned property.

No matter how many times she phoned, I would not go back to 83rd Street for dinner with my mother. The price for this resistance invaded my dreams. For weeks after I'd moved into the apartment, the same dream woke me at three in the morning; my mother, wearing the sunny yellow striped seersucker robe, shrieks and growls at the window of my kitchen fire escape. Her small hands fumble with the latch until she breaks the glass and starts to step through the jagged panes. Just then I awakened in the bedroom off the kitchen. Soaked in sweat, I wasn't convinced I'd dreamt her invasion again. I felt her nails on my neck, but in the gloom (the city is never dark) also saw the rosy geraniums on the fire escape. The nightmare was over one more time. The shakiness ebbed. I took deeper breaths and didn't know it was another panic attack. It was 1960 and *panic attack* was not yet in the language. I was years from being crippled by them. When I called my father at his office to tell him about the dream, he offered to get a locksmith to install an iron window gate but didn't want any dream details. By now he was adept at deflecting the fact that I was overwhelmed because he'd left me with the problem. He went so far as to suggest the invader wasn't Bea at all but really someone else, as if this would reassure me. Despite his usual panic about money, he wanted me calm and not the jittery girl who added to his jitters.

He was willing to pay for the gate. I think he hoped I'd marry within the year and be off his hands, someone else's trouble.

Around Thanksgiving, my father sheepishly admitted he'd been seeing my mother, even taking her on romantic Caribbean weekends. He never asked if the new gate was keeping out the dream. He was dating the problem and walking Buffy again. I was mystified but eager to believe in the fantasy of their reunion.

When I got the Head Start job downtown in Hell's Kitchen, I was excited to be hired without credentials, without training for teaching or preschool day care. I was hired because the director had an unexpected opening and a soft spot for Sarah Lawrence girls. The Tenth Avenue Center sheltered the littlest of children, some of them barely three. It was set up to feed them, let them sleep, and use play as a way of learning. Some of the children were dropped off at seven in the morning and picked up at seven at night. We teachers were only there for eight hours. On my eleven to seven shift, I usually chatted with the mothers after their long work day, their sleepy kids hiding behind them, now suddenly shy, their attachment to us broken by the arrival of their real Moms.

My favorite was Georgie, a Puerto Rican kid whose father was gone and whose mother was hapless and frightened. A spidery little boy of four, Georgie attached himself to me and by attaching gave me confidence, as if he knew something about me that I didn't. At nap time when he stopped his endless wriggling and tossing on the canvas cot, he pulled me down to his lunch stained tee shirt and whispered as he twirled my hair with his sticky fingers, "Hey, Teach,

Teach, you smell good." His eyes half closed, his smile dreamy, this small, whirring machine quieted down although he twitched fitfully in his sleep.

Georgie's Mom was one of the last mothers to show up, and sometimes I was still there when she held his jacket and called to him in Spanish. He streaked around the room until she nearly cried out with exhaustion and complained of the supper she still had to cook. We smiled at each other, and I told her how smart her boy was, trying to give her an incentive not to smack him once they were on the sidewalk.

On the subway ride back uptown, I sifted through my day, separating the high moments from the drudgery. My muscles were sore from lifting kids and equipment, but there were the small triumphs of getting a sullen child to come closer to the reading circle, to smile when his name was called. The canvas cots used for naptime were so much like the ones I'd rested on in the Fours (kindergarten) at The Little Red School House they might as well, be more *madeleines.* Once again I am the small girl waiting for her Mom after school, racing around in front of the school's entrance, ignoring her pleas... back with my mother who, even if she isn't paying attention, isn't snarling.

The subway platform was deserted at my 23rd Street stop. I moved quickly towards the empty staircase. (Only later will I remember the jaundiced yellow of the man's cheeks who'd sat across from me, staring.) When I felt his hands under my skirt, grabbing my thighs, I swung my purse into his face, amazed at the sound of my own scream. He turned and bolted down the stairs, disappearing before the turnstile clerk appeared at my side. The police took down my description and told me to forget it, to get to my job. It will be years before I put together my grandfather's heart attack, those thick hands on my skin and my fear of being underground or in close spaces. Only now I see how I *etched* trauma, bronzed the baby shoe, memorized the details instead of letting whatever it was, go. Might phobia be the ultimate generalization—swallowing one bad clam and freezing the frame?

I was having dizzy spells in the subway (there was no other way to get downtown in less than an hour), walking along the side of buildings, or in supermarkets under bright fluorescents. When I'd had anxiety attacks in the Sarah Lawrence years, no one called them that. I had been high-strung, nervous, too nervous, but now anxiety was the title for weak-kneed episodes that were increasing.

Late one afternoon my father left an urgent message at my Center. "Your mother is in my office!" By the time I got to his building on Madison Avenue and off the elevator, the police were leaving her to the ambulance attendant. Tied down on a stretcher, her purse laid across her stomach, she was bellowing, "Liar! Salesman! Goddamn salesman!"

The office staff behaved as if they hadn't seen her tossing papers and pencils to the floor as if she was in her own living room. They bowed their heads and moved back to their offices. No one greeted me. It was as if they were giving me a pass, letting me disappear. My father's face was ashen, the same pallor as at my graduation. He motioned me to the foot of the stretcher, out of her sight. We didn't look at her or at each other. He whispered as if we could be disturbing a movie audience, signaling me to follow behind the stretcher.

"Go, go with her... she's going Upstate... you know."

"Dad, I can't!... I can't go again, not me! You get in there!" I hissed at him fiercely, but we both knew I couldn't refuse the guy who'd put up the gate, who'd carried me out of the bathtub... the father who wasn't nuts, just weak.

"There's nothing to do. Just go... someone has to!"

Once again, I'm to be the one on the jump seat. As we sped along Madison Avenue, her murmur brought me close to her cheek, to the straps holding her arms tightly. A straitjacket wasn't a jacket at all, just a padded vest with buckles and snaps.

"Listen, please listen... " Her eyes darted from side to side, as we flew through darkness.

We were alone with a stranger. I was afraid she'd choke on the spittle dribbling off the side of her mouth but more afraid to blot it, to touch her.

"I know what's going on... I know what he's up to... " She spoke as if they were still together, but, in fact, they have been apart for almost a year, his little dating game long past. Before I could remind her of this detail, her head lolled to one side, and she stopped talking. She'd been up for forty-eight hours and now, in the speeding ambulance, was taking a long-needed nap.

The next day at the Center, the spider song, the reading circle, the hugs and kisses at nap time held me fast, kept me steady, despite replaying the ride, my attempt at a farewell kiss at Pinewood and her words as she turned her face and was wheeled away. One last punch did find its usual mark,

"We're not such good friends anyway."

By the end of the day I couldn't stop imaging the yellow house where they were electroshocking her, jolting her back. I saw her strapped down for the injection, saw the gauze wrapped around her jaw, the contraption around her skull and pinned to her temples. Putting myself in her place was the least I could do. For no matter how much she derailed me, with rejection and seductions I longed for reunion—craziness erased, the soft mother back again.

I can't know then that magical thinking isn't something you can dip in and out of. Rather, it is honed until it is so automatic that you won't know for years how it blurred your vision; how for much of your life, you'll remove your glasses to blur the moment, to remain in the doorway—myopia as metaphor.

My cousin Roy agreed to stay at the apartment so Buffy could be home, not at a kennel. It seemed practical and better for Buffy to have Roy's regular schedule, not the long hours I was spending at the Center. Besides, I had Sybil and Simon. This arrangement with Roy was a relief and solved the problem. Although I still thought of Buffy at odd moments or when I saw another golden spaniel pulling its owner down the block, he'd begun to fade for me, the way pets do when you go to college and they become your parents' animal. That little blond guy had been upstaged by the sheer excitement of my new life.

By the third day of my mother's hospitalization, I couldn't concentrate on anything I was supposed to be doing with the children at the Center. Their voices were far away and the routine a mystery, as if I had learned nothing and could teach nothing. At nap time it seemed like a good idea to close my eyes, too, but as soon as I stretched out on an empty cot, tears streaked my cheeks. I held my arm across my wet face. The children sighed in their light sleep, their small bodies curled on the cots, their legs tucked up to their chests.

Don't let Georgie see me like this, I begged the ceiling. I'm his reliable person, who must be steady. The Center's director came to my cot and firmly helped me up. Guiding me to her office where she will call my father, I passed the children deep in sleep or dozing and am relieved they haven't seen me as crumpled as they can be when they lose whatever little moorings they have.

As we traveled uptown in a cab, my father put his arm around my shoulders tentatively, as though it was the thing to do under the circumstances of collecting his grown daughter from her job. I was mortified to be taken away from the children and didn't say a word all the way to 70th Street.

For a week I stayed in the apartment, unable to tell Gail, who was spending half her time at her boyfriend's, or anyone else, what was happening to me. I wasn't being purposefully mysterious. I didn't know why I collapsed or why I couldn't just go back to my job, to my kids. If my mother had died, my sobbing and nausea would have been expected. But because she was locked up at Pinewood, getting shock treatments in the little yellow cottage, I was keeping a secret which was making me sick.

I got dressed, at the end of the day, when my father arrived with supper. As he warmed up the food for his loony daughter and made small talk about the office, did he wish he was at his orderly drawing board, instead of juggling pans while I sat silently at the table? Once the food was warm and set between us, he concentrated on chewing. Was he as spooked as I was by how much I seemed like my mother when she was depressed? Was this the first time I wasn't Teddy's daughter and now was Bea's girl?

As he went down the stairs, my father looked back and smiled his Brooklyn Bridge smile, hand in the air for his usual exit. I longed, in that moment, to chase down after him, to ask if I could go back with him, go home. But staying with him was out of the question now that his apartment was shared with the "stranger" who was, unbeknownst to me, about to become my stepmother after their Mexican wedding, after the Mexican divorce he'd initiated on his last surprise visit to Pinewood. My mother had described how relieved she'd been to see him, back again, back to her. But he hadn't sat down or taken off his coat.

"You know how he is ... he kept his hands in his pocket until he whipped it out like a box of Crackerjacks ... the divorce papers!"

How could I tell the kids at the center I was leaving them? That I was like their Dads who suddenly evaporated or their Moms, who disappeared into drugs or booze, that I was to be another missing person. I'd felt indispensable, the teacher who truly got them, knew all their loco tricks and had ways to soothe them when they needed to come down from hilarity or drama. Now I wouldn't get to see their clay bugs painted or their puppets stapled together for the parent show. But mostly I wouldn't get to hold them on my lap until they lay back and their heads were tucked beneath my chin.

18

My father's graduation present came a year after the June event, and only after I'd proven I could earn a living, even if I did have to quit the Center. My trip to Europe was not given as the frivolous gambit my WASP classmates expected. Just as these girls had shown me their world of entitlement, they'd also shown me how my foot went too quickly to the brake. I was no match for the sheer careless fun of their escapades.

With a newly remarried, tightfisted father and a mother who was not getting any better, my post-collegiate madcap trip was not as daring as it seemed. I was way too worried about leaving my mother with no one but my cousin Roy for emergencies. I had visions of police cars, ambulances, and no one to interpret for my mother who would be incapable of speaking in full sentences. The tug of war took hold: to go or to stay, to have the adventure or to mind my mother.

Miraculously, as plans needed to be made, my mother, set loose again from Pinewood, found a job at a doctor's office on the East Side. Against all odds, a pediatrician hired her to be his receptionist. She was in a good period, smoothed out and still pretty, looking refined in crepe blouses. When she dies, I tell myself, my mother will go, not to Heaven, but to the Lord & Taylor blouse department in the sky.

My European itinerary was planned around the young men who'd encouraged my visits: Benjamin in Paris and Leonard in Greece. Although some of my classmates had married and others were promised, I was sure I wasn't eligible for the protected lives they will lead. It wasn't that I was so devilishly sexy. I was hysterical and convinced, by my father, that no one would marry the daughter of a mad woman.

Hours after arriving in Paris, Benjamin installed me in an apartment his parents kept for guests, just above Givenchy's salon on Avenue George V. Benjamin was another Central Park West boy, with intense dark looks and international credentials: his father, Avram, was an Israeli who'd fought with the right-wing Urgun in '48, his mother, Gloria, spoke three languages and moved seamlessly between their apartments in New York, Paris, and Tel Aviv. I was so eager for motherly approval that Gloria's acceptance of me, if not her enthusiasm, was enough for the moment. It will be from her I'll get a glimpse of how it works: how a middle-aged woman kept her allure. Besides the face powder that was hand-mixed for her, she spent one day a week in her bed. Not ill, just lying prone so water left her ankles, and puffiness never took up permanent residence in her cheeks.

Benjamin had other crucial information for me: as we sat at a cafe on the Champs-Elysees, he explained the difference between *frais du bois* and regular strawberries. The small ones from the woods were delicacies, prized for their tart sweetness. Our plates were filled with mounds of *crème fraîche* covering the deep red berries. Together, he pointed out, the combination was legendary. With Benjamin at my

166

side, his dark eyes piercing mine, those legends became mine. What I could do for Benjamin, who was three years younger, was dispel his worry about still being a virgin.

In those weeks on Avenue Georges V, I was welcomed into the Baums' world, where his father's whispered Israeli phone calls were taken within earshot of the dinner table, where Gloria's insistence that lavender was a color, distinct from lilac, was considered a topic, where champagne was usual, and glamour, as familiar as her perfume, was in the air.

Benjamin and I took turns guiding one another around. He knew Paris as if it were New York, and I knew just enough about our bodies to give him confidence. On my weekly trips to American Express, where I waited in line to find, once more, that my mother hadn't written, he was just right, holding me against his jacket until I stopped trembling.

"She's probably locked up again. That's why there's no letter," I whispered.

It was better to imagine the worst, there in the American Express, nearly a replica of the Sistine Chapel, than to risk a transatlantic call, which would cost amazing amounts of money and bring her into the middle of the Baum's damask-lined salon.

Benjamin walked me through Paris with his arm round my shoulders, his lanky gait slowed to mine. Because of his true knack for empathy, I confessed that my mother's whereabouts, in or out of a hospital, had become an *accompaniment, a* faint but steady beat wherever I was. What I couldn't know at twenty three, was that this kind of distraction has the power to make you an observer in the doorway, instead of a participant.

Just as I had stood in the doorway when Levita brought tea to my raving mother, I was still in the doorway, even, if it seemed, I was having one adventure after another. It would take being in Paris to discover that even thousands of miles away, I'd not gone far enough. She was under my skin, a steady beat, beat, beat.

The plan had always been to go on to Greece. Months before, after four years of silence and on a few hours notice, Leonard had come to 70th Street for an evening, drinking tea at my kitchen table in front of the blue wall. There was no flirtation. He'd mostly spoken of the novel he was working on (it was to be *Beautiful Losers*), characteristically asked no questions about my life and so it was a surprise when he'd turned round on the staircase, smiling, and murmured, "Come, come to Hydra... " then disappeared down the shadowy stairs, leaving me to replay that weekend at his studio Kasbah, in Montreal, where he'd proclaimed his love for women who were as beautiful as gypsies.

I arranged to meet my opera-loving college friend, Fay, at the third-class hotel in Athens we could afford. After a few days of sightseeing, she agreed to come along to Hydra. I didn't know where Leonard lived or whether I was still welcome, but with Fay beside me, I was trying on *cheeky,* able to dare because I didn't expect to find him. In a dimly lit grocery store, I asked the proprietor if he knew the Canadian Leonard Cohen—just as the stooped poet appeared in the doorway. He greeted me as if we had an appointment. His hug and measured step was the choreography I remembered, the hushed tone hypnotic. If there was any surprise, I would never know.

The three of us had coffee on the café's terrace, as if we've run into each other on an errand. Fay observed him as she might an exotic leopard. I was surprisingly at ease with Leonard's absence as presence, having learned it at my mother's knee. The time at Pripstein's and in Montreal, was imprinted. As beautiful as gypsies... was enough to carry me along. Like so many young women who've discovered literature in time to title their experience, I wanted to see where the story went.

Fay shared my pension room for a day or so and decided to return to New York. I glided into the non-decision to remain on the island. As we waited for the hydrofoil at the wharf, she cheered me on like a guide who'd taken her charge as far as she could and reminded me that my real life was in New York. Years later, I will describe my one white dress, the embroidered bag and a few cosmetics I'd brought to the island. If I'd brought more from the Athens hotel, it would have spoiled the story.

Had Leonard said "come to Hydra" without ever dreaming I might do just that? Once there, in his sparsely furnished white house, we could have been back in that Montreal weekend, four years before. When I showered in the dirt-floored basement, Leonard rinsed me off with buckets of water warmed by the sun, as if I were his child. When we had suppers with his Australian mates, Charmian and George Johnson, they wrongfully assumed we were lovers. I was waiting for declaration, but instead there was the same kind of pantomime he'd created in his Montreal studio. I was no match for whatever mysterious game Leonard was playing. What I could do was to leave on the quay of Hydra's crescent-shaped harbor the troubles I'd dumped on Benjamin in Paris—as I walked the steep steps up to Leonard's house, determined to keep my mother at bay.

For those weeks, I was not in the middle of her movie, but rather, at the end of a sun bleached day, at a table with Leonard, encircled with intense expat talk and occasional bursts of song—on furlough. Out of Bea's reach, I roamed the island on my own, sitting for hours at the water's edge, inventing my new path without imagining the detours. And yes, I washed and wore that same white batiste dress for two weeks, and made a point of not buying anything but a bathing suit.

Hydra's white walls, navy sea, dusty cobbles would be memorized in a way that, a few years later, will be equaled only by the palette of Mexico. In that shadowless Greek light, I was bedazzled but not informed. Mistakenly, place will prevail; color and vista will become balm—as if the setting could provide the protection I was looking for instead of risking taking flight without a net. Allowing myself to be as beautiful as a gypsy?

Leonard and I waited at the hydrofoil dock, the choreography reprising our meeting weeks before. Charmian and George had come down to see me off and stood behind us, nearly parental. Wordlessly, he held me against his chest (as he will four years later in New York when he finds me again) and silently smiled his goodbye. I walked onto the gangplank as if I were boarding the Madison Avenue bus, as the Johnsons sang out, "Come back, come back, come back!"

When the boat picked up speed, I could no longer see him waving. It was 1961, a few years before the poet, will become the singer-songwriter, who will create the legendary "Suzanne" and make a life with Marianne and her young son on the island, after my time in his white walled sanctuary.

I continued on to Tel Aviv to see friends I'd met in New York. When the customs officer looked up, and before taking my passport, said, "Welcome home," I was bedazzled, seduced by instant inclusion. The seven-year-old girl who'd longed for her usual Christmas tree was nowhere in sight.

A few days later, jammed between fellow commuters on a train to Haifa, "Welcome Home" returned. Instead of claustrophobic, I felt connected. Might I not be as alone as I'd always felt? This moment was just a moment and won't hold, when panic attacks will make me feel I don't belong to myself, let alone to a tribe.

Before returning to New York, I met Collin in London. We'd been writing, and I couldn't leave Europe without seeing him, although my father had joined me in Rome and insisted on coming to London. He was staying in the same hotel, a few floors from my room. Only later would it occur to me that his presence was part of the odds stacked against us. Although the white dress remained at the bottom of my suitcase, the film of the days with Leonard ran as we, finally, made an attempt to be lovers, not the frantic teenagers fumbling on the sofa. But I'd been seduced by poetry, not the balladeer I'd left on the dock . . . so when we finally could be lovers, we couldn't read each other on the crisp hotel sheets. Both of us had moved too far from our days in Montreal.

When he left my room and crept down the hall to his, despite urging me to come to Sardinia where his Oxford friends had rented a villa, where we might have discovered more about our post-collegiate selves—the movie we'd always made, was over.

When I am trapped in the Brooklyn brownstone, in the marriage, it is Collin, not Leonard, who will appear in dream and daydream: that first evening in sub-zero Montreal winter, our cheeks frozen, our lips bruised as we kissed beneath the street lamp, lavender sachets in a linen closet, a brick house protected by stone lions on the stoop, always at the movies, never having put to the test... a life together. When he became a political public figure in England, friends reassured me that it wouldn't have worked.

19

"When you speak to your butcher I'm tempted to grab the phone and tell the poor guy to hold two turtledove eggs and a wren's wing for you." Sanford Ware was a staff writer at *Esquire,* who'd been spying on me for months and knew a tricky charmer when he saw one. My five o'clock phone calls to the butcher, on Second Avenue, must have seemed oddly luxurious for a lowly editorial researcher, fact checker. It was just so convenient to call in our order and have it ready when Gail or I appeared at the store, our arms always filled.

If at twenty-four I am so highly specific, Sanford wanted to know where I was headed, how could I soar? He never asked me out but continued to tease me as I learned to fact-check and do original research for writers. Fact-checking an article was a relief at first. I loved sleuthing, being on the trail of what could be verified. Nothing left to interpretation, unless flagged as such. Every word counted, unlike those that had been thrown around by my mother carelessly, deadly as grenades.

In the middle of a busy morning, as I was happily parsing a sentence, my cousin Roy called. "Are you busy?" His voice had that soft anxious tone that I recognized as meaning he needed to interrupt. This had to be about Bea.

"It's okay. What's up?" I wished I'd not answered, not left my challenging sentence.

"This is going to sound crazy, . . ." his voice broke, with small gagging sounds.

I hated his exaggerated reactions to my mother. She was bad enough but his being both baffled and resigned annoyed me. I wanted him to take a stand against her absurd demands, even if I could not.

"More than usual?" I asked.

That last episode, when I'd been called at the Center, had happened, just down Madison, at my father's office. That ambulance ride was as etched as all the others, the feeling in my body could come flooding back if I let it in.

"She wants me to take Buffy to the vet," he whispered. "She thinks he causes your Dad's asthma. She wants to . . ."

"His asthma is better because he's away from her, not Buffy." I interrupted, getting into the problem like so many other times we'd tried to figure out what she was up to. Roy was my cousin and kind of my brother—in and out of our house all these years, almost a sibling.

"It's worse than that. She thinks Ted will come back if Buffy is gone. She's going to have him put to sleep." He choked out the words.

A rushing, roaring wind flooded my ears. My tongue swelled, temples pulsed. I held onto the edge of my desk, cold sweat breaking beneath my blouse.

"She's what?"

"Putting him to sleep. She says he has to be out of the picture. I'm taking him this afternoon at five." He replied flatly as if he'd already accepted his role in this "errand," this murder of hers. He had caved in so many times, trying to please my mother, the aunt he'd loved from childhood and now feared.

I said I had to hang up, had to figure this out. I implied that I'd be calling him back. As the afternoon wore on, I moved like a sleepwalker through the manuscript. A few months before, I'd rushed from the Center, had obeyed my father and stepped into the ambulance with my tied-down mother. A good, reliable girl, unable to protect myself then and now on this October afternoon, unable to protect Buffy, told Roy to bring him to me so I could take him home to my place.

Why didn't I race across town and up to 83rd Street? Why did I let my healthy dog be murdered? The fact of having two cats at my place hasn't been part of this picture no matter how many times I've rewritten it. I want to believe that there was real doubt that my mother would go through with such a crazy plan, and that that doubt kept me watching the clock, transfixed, but not moving. But I am more inclined to believe that in those years, I was only *half-present*, so frozen that staying in my chair, as if nothing were happening, was more possible than impossible—the existence of Sybil and Simon a detail.

I don't remember leaving the office or coming back to my apartment that evening. Only Roy's tight, flat zombie voice remains as if he, too, had taken leave of his senses and was part of my mother's picture. It will be many years before I connect my dog-rescuing days to that afternoon. As I write this, Buffy's peanut butter smell returns—imagining him, jauntily pulling my cousin down the street, that sparkling fall day.

20

"You are much too smart and much too lovely to be buried in the stacks." I'd heard a variation of this line since I came to work with writers, those young men in corduroy who hung around the editorial department. This time the line had more authority, in a British accent, as Philip Daley peered down my dress. We were a few hours into a book party, where, as the evening went on, playful banter was replaced with penetrating, staring contests. The mood in the room had shifted. The last of the food was gone, and lipstick stained glasses were left half full. Suddenly there was a rush to leave, to go off into the night.

I knew Philip's byline and the acclaim he'd won in only a few years of publishing, I'd even read his long-winded, comma-laded pieces on inland waterways. The ones on boat building I'd ignored. I'm aware of being noticed when we leave the party arm-in-arm, as if we're already lovers.

Once settled in the cab, Philip leaned towards me, both audaciously and deferentially, the emboldened school boy still minding his manners. His large suntanned hands were more masculine than his face, which was cheerfully Anglo-Irish, less than chiseled, a rosy cheeked boyishness atop a grown man's long body. Into the night Philip told sea stories, danced me around my kitchen, and undressed me more slowly than anyone ever had. His assurance was irresistible. It included having the grace to be properly chagrined the next morning, at breakfast, when he confessed that his wife and three little girls were at home on the Maryland shore and that his marriage, in these early Sixties, was called an "open marriage."

"I don't know... if I can do this," I said. We considered the possibility of not going on and then fell into each other's arms, our mouths sticky with marmalade.

We met when we could, often without much notice, as if we were meeting in wartime. His urgent phone calls added to the excitement. As he burst through my doorway, his cheeks were as flushed as if he'd been sailing. Philip was always in high gear, and that gear carried us along.

One fall evening he arrived in a rainstorm and held me against his slicker, kissing my eyelids.

"Your hands are sooo cold," I whispered, as if we were in a public place.

"Windows wouldn't come up... three hours in the rain." He was impersonating a gallant officer, ". . . hands frozen to the wheel, hurrying to be with you, against all odds."

I could see those builder hands on the tiller of his beloved boat, guiding it through the harbor. I wanted to freeze the frame of us standing in my doorway, my hands on his, his mouth on mine. I was memorizing him as I sensed him memorizing me when we lay together. The difference was that I held the images between visits, and he moved back into a life crowded with other pictures.

Our mornings were too short for the languid, somewhat tortured farewell I'd have liked and were heavy with daylight guilt. When I dressed for work, inventing myself, I chose my costumes as carefully as a baker weighing his flour. I sucked in my cheeks and covered my round breasts with deepest purples, bloodiest garnets.

If Philip was tense and remote, I was impatient to have the apartment to myself, to put myself together for work, applying mascara as if my life depended on it. With the deliberate strokes of a pointillist, I banished the queasy, spacey feeling that morning brought and wished he didn't whistle going down the stairs as he did coming up in the evening. I wanted some sign that he left me affected if not changed. My Jewish heart was trying to be just *nicked* by the Goyim, not broken. How easily they came and went, whistling down the stairs!

In the evenings, I'd tear bits and pieces off the chicken we'd had the night before. As I drank the last of our wine, I realized how happy I'd been cooking and waiting for Philip. Twenty-four hours later, I could be content with the reverie of him, despite flashes of longing, content that he was there with me again, encircling me as I'd cooked, distracting with embraces and dance steps.

As I nibbled and smelled tarragon, I twirled in the middle of the room. I didn't know then that *remembering* was to become my *specialite´* or that nostalgia could grip me, even before there was a *past* to be recalled. I was modeling myself to be the perfect mistress of the moderately known author. If I could be satisfied with recall, between our moments of reunion, we would keep on.

I imagined Philip carrying back to Maryland the gingham his wife, Candice, needed for curtains which we'd found on one of our Lower East Side prowls. He'd actually asked for my advice. I had known where to take him and found the Orchard Street bargain for his Maryland kitchen. I told myself to enjoy the gentle irony of his Saab barreling along the Jersey Turnpike with bolts of cloth we'd chosen together. In some bizarre way this included me in his real life.

Without admitting resentment or envy at the snugness of his family, the three little girls at the table in front of the yellow gingham, I chose to worry about his ancient car, instead of worrying about when we would meet again. I didn't know that Philip would always have an ancient Saab, no matter how much success came to him. His affectations were still lost on me. In those first months, I was like someone swimming dreamily underwater, cut off from the voices on the shore. Even before Phillip described Candice to me, in the kind of detail which made her real, I'd invented her. I'd see her standing at the beach which jutted into the bay, sharp stones faintly marking, not actually cutting her bare feet. In my tableaux, she was a woman of a hundred years before, waiting for her husband, expecting him to wrap her in Chinese silk he'd carried for months at sea. Whereas I was the native girl, the maiden he left behind, under palms in the South Pacific.

I could have drawn a map of their seaside village and described the sounds of the harbor. With Philip as my guide, I saw all too easily the village square, as fixed for him as his children, who waited for his homecomings and curled round his legs, as he crossed their porch. It seemed peculiar to be given the details so specifically, so carelessly and it made me not trust him to protect Candice, nor me. He seemed capable of leading me one pearly evening, to his beloved Rocky Point, to lie entwined, to be discovered.

I was sure that Candice held their family together. The devoted wife of the transplanted British writer, supporting him in his career, agreeing to any travel assignment that would pass for the adventure his life was meant to be. Without her agreement (had they, in fact, ever negotiated the terms of their marriage?), how would he trip the light fantastic, how would he manage his Fred Astaire routine? He said enough for me to guess that no amount of wine could make Candice dance with him in public, that long ago she'd found a way of hardly moving at all, if he did pull her to her feet at a party. But when the children were asleep, she would happily embrace him. He wanted me to know that she was not a cold woman. She just couldn't join the wide angle of his dance. He wanted me to see that his pursuit of me, his race to the top of my stairs, was out of a lavishness he expected from life, not because he was lacking at home. This self-description seemed to reassure him just as it allowed me to enjoy him as I had never enjoyed anyone before. I could be with him, without measuring him for a permanent fit.

When Philip wasn't restless and planning the next delivery of a boat to Bermuda, I knew he reveled in family domesticity, involving himself in all the daily details: scanning grocery ads and neatly tearing out the sale coupons to be stored in his beloved Mark Cross wallet, trotting off for school pick ups, checking the local dry goods store for sale sneakers, and when friends' babies were born knocking on neighbors' doors to spread the news. Wasn't this why they had forsaken city life for a village where they could tell their neighbors the good and the bad; a Chesapeake Bay village that would be made famous when his book was published to warm reviews.

And when he packed his canvas bag and stood in their doorway, with it slung over his shoulder, I imagined Candice sensing he wasn't with them anymore, his blue eyes not meeting hers. He had that way of taking off as if he were already gone. I couldn't believe it was unique to my doorway. He could have said to either of us, "Ta…" as he grinned and left.

As his train streaked towards the city, leaving behind the hills of the countryside and coming closer to the glossy shrubbery of the suburbs, I imagined his pulse beginning its adventure beat. He enjoyed being part of the rush-hour throng at Baltimore's Penn Station, knowing he wouldn't be returning at five. He was also thankful not to be in a business suit, to be in his L.L. Bean bush jacket, and to have arranged his life so he could do as he pleased most of the time.

Without the grandiose ambition or the gnawing self-doubt of his friends writing fiction, he had narrowed his sights and made a safe place for himself. A detached, ardent observer, he wrote books which were never about himself or even other people but were about delivering boats and sailing his own. Country living completed a perfect balance, giving him the double pleasure of living there but having the excuse to leave when larger libraries were needed for the authenticity critics had come to expect, or when he was just inexplicably restless.

That fall belonged to me, or so he said, as if he could offer me a whole season, if not a whole life.

In bed, he put his hands under my hips and lifted me against him, murmuring,

"You're marvelous, simply marvelous."

At breakfast, buttering his toast, he said solemnly, "I'm quite consumed with you." He said *consumed* as if he'd been waiting years to use the word.

Each time we met, I reminded myself to be as irreverent and playful as the first time. Our few hours were to be spent nestling, praising the way we fit together. I was determined not to be overly serious, the yearning girl tripping him up. I almost never answered the phone when he was with me on our South Sea Island. But one evening, as I was carrying dinner to the table, it rang. I'd been dodging my mother's calls all day at the office and knew this was another of hers.

"Let it go! "Philip lowered his voice to a playful growl, "Won't share you with anyone tonight!"

The more I wished for another Mother, the more I wished her to disappear, the more power she had. Handing him the fragrant dish, I picked up the phone.

"Let me tell you something! Important! ... a dream of your father ... we're dancing ... a rumba!"

"Mom ... I'm busy ... tomorrow, I'll call you in the morning."

"Morning!" She sang out and tumbled on, as Philip slipped his arm around my waist.

"When you get your ass to the phone, I'll be dead!" She slammed the receiver down. I saw her redialing even before I put mine down.

I took the phone off the hook and turned into Philip's arms. I was torn, as always, between her drama or living my own. Until now,

I'd edited my mother out with Philip, unwilling to risk the truth of her with him. He didn't ask for an explanation, but held me against his chest, moving as if there was music, hummed a bar or two, and opened the wine. I took the comfort of him and didn't wonder if he was tactful or just detached. Being divided was an old story I'd learned to ignore. If I'd taken any high school Latin I might have known the roots of family and familiar are the same. I might have made the connections which would have kept me from attaching to those divided, ambivalent, unavailable.

All of which is ahead of me and not in my kitchen that fall, dancing cheek to cheek with someone else's husband.

Clips of Philip's life carried me from one evening to another: Philip striding through airports, unfettered, on the prowl, work meshing with curiosity; Philip bound to his daily rounds, ritual as romance.

He told of putting his youngest girl on the potty in the middle of the night, as if to say I can do all the usual things when I'm not having an adventure. He preferred Conrad to Mailer, could actually build a boat as well as sail it. Disparagingly, he dismissed Virginia Woolf, one of my idols, as another of those "self indulgent ladies" and asked, "I mean, you're going to *do* things, aren't you?"

It was as if he saw the brakes, the still-life, that could make me a spectator. He believed people could be enchanted with words *and* running, jumping, moving, moving through their time, never bound.

One morning as we were finishing breakfast, Philip leaned forward, elbows on the table, his hand under my chin. With the other, he traced the bridge of my nose as if he were sketching and said softly, "Do you know what I love about sailing? It gives the same clarity you get from a camera... I can place the exact line of the horizon."

I didn't know why he was bringing to breakfast the talk we might have at dinner, when there was a whole night before us—until he held my face in both hands and said, "I need that clarity. And I'm losing it with you." He covered his own face with his hands and whispered, "Each time I go back, it gets harder."

A few days later, Philip's phone voice was in the *vibrato* emergency that I'd first found beguiling, but now was somewhat suspect. "I'm off to the Everglades tomorrow! Can we have tonight?" I wasn't drawn in as usual and made my tea measuring the leaves instead of tossing them into the pot, as if by slowing down I might discover what I felt. His call had broken into my dream: a house of many rooms, flooded with light, each window framing a meadow.

I drew heavy lines across my sleep swollen lids and chose a magenta shawl to protect me from the November chill at the bus stop. I wanted to be going to the Everglades, too, or at least not downtown to *Esquire*, confined from nine to five, fixing other people's sentences. I was restless in the work and still mixed up about work and *Eros*—as if *Eros* could be the antidote for a life poisoned with dread, with the ever present worry of where Bea was and what she was doing. Except when attraction took the wheel, and that drama overruled the one I'd been minding for years. And in fairness, Bea was not the only reason for my falling too easily into bed. It was the Sixties, and permission had been given to those of us not promised, not already Moms.

After a Hungarian dinner on Second Avenue, Philip guided me purposefully back to my apartment. Crushed against his slicker, I was enveloped in his warmth which usually took my breath away.

"I feel marvelous! . . . couldn't ask for more . . . the night with you, tomorrow catching up with that boat!" He swept me off my feet and, yes, carried me across my own threshold, setting me down in the kitchen.

I moved quickly past the tiny bedroom to the living room, to be farthest from our dancing meals, farthest from our rumpled bed.

"Won't you be here with me?" Philip patted the sofa, smiling quizzically. We'd had slivovitz and the warmth was still with him.

"I'm thinking of leaving my job." I said slowly, for emphasis.

He sank against the pillows and then leaned forward earnestly, his broad shoulders straining the blue denim work shirt he'd worn for the new assignment.

"Must it be decided tonight, just when I want you uncomplicated and laughing?"

I knew this script and the childlike smoothness of his back, the slope of his shoulders when he moved away from our bed, and I plowed ahead anyway.

"I want to go . . . maybe a job in Europe. I want to be the one who goes, not always the one who stays." Was I purposefully misleading him, having him believe it was the world I wanted and not him? Or was I looking for an exit to save myself the hard fall I sensed was coming?

"Well then," he murmured, "we must celebrate your new intentions."

Reprieved from a place I was unsure of, we made love like our first time, before I learned he belonged to someone else.

"Philip."

"Yes, luv, what is it?" We'd had a hasty breakfast and he was struggling with his canvas pack, stowing his gear.

"I always see your girls, flying into your arms. They wait for you..." Before I could finish he was beside me.

"It's not a contest." He bent to put his lips to my neck. "I want everything... and you're right. I'm with them even before I smell the water."

His eyes were bright, nearly glistening. For what he was about to lose? For Candice, who at that moment could be preparing stew for the girls' dinner? But mostly for himself, for his restlessness—for those pieces of himself, he often said, couldn't be brought together—for the gnawing unease he'd felt since he was a small boy, even before being shipped away from the London bombings.

"Well, yes," he cleared his throat, as if in summation, "I don't know why I expected us to go on and on." He grinned, his most rueful, boyish grin. "Allow me the maudlin... the best things aren't meant to."

I put my palm against his cheek as if we both knew I was already becoming the girl *remembered.*

"You're right, of course," his accent more clipped than ever,"... quite so, quite so. You know more than I do. Always did."

For the last time, he traced the bridge of my nose with his thumb. I was tempted to take back the scene, to tamp down my rebellion which was ending us. But he was gripping his bag.

"You won't be seeing the likes of me so soon again," he exclaimed dramatically, and then with his back to me and without drama, murmured, "And I won't be seeing the likes of you either...."

21

Breaking with Philip didn't send me into the wide world or even to the Europe I wanted to trade for a life without him. But it got me to tell Clay Felker, features editor of *Esquire* (and about to create *New York Magazine*), that I wanted to leave my job and needed freelance work to have more time to write. Clay paid attention and one afternoon introduced me to the two German magazine men who would change my life. Their publication was *Twen,* and their audience was readers in their twenties who'd been children during the war. The art director and the editor were looking for an American to rep them in New York and to interview celebrities of interest to young Germans.

Working for *Twen* was like getting a grant. Suddenly there was time to write the post-collegiate novel (which would remain in a drawer), to dart around the city in wool suits instead of shawls, to meet the American counterparts of my German employers. The West German Press Office, created to show a contrite post-war Germany to the world, sponsored our parties at their Goethe House on Fifth Avenue, across from the Metropolitan Museum, their stodgy director standing nearly at attention as I introduced Hans and Willy to their Madison Avenue counterparts. Doing interviews with Anthony Quinn, Jane Fonda, Lotte Lenya, Philip Roth and more was part of the deal, even when Lenya had to show me how to use my tape recorder, after she'd brought out salami and champagne.

I was a twenty-five-year-old *pisher*, wheeling and dealing as if these negotiations were dinner parties on 70th Street. I sent invitations without RSVP and never knew who'd climb the staircase to Goethe House's second floor. When Theodore Bikel showed up, he was not coming like a lamb to the Germans, but sang out "Good evening" as he lifted me into the air, made one full turn, and set me back onto the marble parquet grinning and waving to the guests on the balcony.

Without leaving 70th Street, I'd embarked. If Philip's trips were literally on water, mine were into a heady world where people were rewarded for accomplishment. My attention was too divided to complete the novel. Instead, there was "the pursuit of *Eros*," as Marcy had nailed it, getting other freelance magazine assignments, and keeping Bea out of state mental hospitals, now that my father was no longer paying for her stays at private ones. (In the Sixties a state facility could mean permanent confinement.)

I didn't tell my mother, who had moved into a building two blocks from mine, that I had this connection to the Goethe House right there on Fifth Avenue, walking distance from her apartment. I was spending wit and energy keeping her at bay. Gail and I still spent evenings in my blue-walled kitchen, proclaiming the virtues of the perfect sofa as a metaphor for the perfect life. One rainy spring night I held the teapot in mid-air, transported to one of my beloved Bloomsbury drawing rooms and proclaimed archly, as if to an assembled cognoscenti,

"It's obvious... there's never any sexual drama in Eden."

As Gail moved towards marriage, I dreamt up the capitals of Europe or at least imagined a return to Paris. My wish for escape

189

had no real direction. It was an amorphous desire, like being vaguely hungry but not knowing what to eat, what would satisfy.

One morning in early April, the phone rang. I was steeled for another Bea emergency but instead the German Information Office was asking if I would fill in for Chicago's Mayor Daley, who was too ill to take his Berlin press junket. Before I could get my breath, they asked if I wanted an interview with Chancellor Willy Brandt, or instead, a cultural itinerary to see how West Germany was reclaiming itself as a civilized nation twenty years after the War. The "cultural itinerary" was my choice. Willy Brandt was unimaginable, even for a young woman who was always daring herself.

I had two weeks to prepare a trip that should have taken many more. The Press Office invited me for a three-week tour, and I tacked on some weeks in Paris to see Franny and her new husband. I imagined the boulevards of springtime Berlin with its famous linden trees in flower, but didn't anticipate how newly constructed buildings, next to bombed out ruins, would remind me of how the Germans had suffered and that being in West Germany, just twenty years after the Holocaust, would tell me I was a Jew, albeit one who'd been safely playing after school, in Washington Square as the camps were being filled, the Final Solution carried out.

A meeting with Chancellor Brandt would have been *in context*, part of a whole picture I wasn't focused on, in order to accept the invitation. Was never seeing the whole picture, as my nursery school Rorschach revealed, my permanent default?

My agent, who'd been getting me occasional magazine assignments, scrambled to get me one for Berlin. Why not an interview with Günter Grass, West Germany's literary lion? If I had a specific assignment, the Press Office would get me an interview with one of the most famous writers in Europe. Without the assignment, I was just another hopeful young woman trying to get an audience with the literary pope, who had just won every important prize in Europe for *The Tin Drum*.

The night before my departure, Gail gave the party. That April evening was mild, without the usual bite before spring in New York. The stairwell was filled with friends coming to wish me well; my floor through rocked with high spirits. A somewhat mad Swiss film producer I'd recently invited to the Goethe House burst into the kitchen declaring his love for me: "... we will meet in Paris," he promised before he stumbled out as suddenly as he'd stumbled in.

My father and stepmother made a brief appearance because they knew Bea wasn't invited. She and I had said our goodbyes at a restaurant on Madison. I'd watched my mother walk up the avenue, presentable in her tweed suit, looking like any other matron going home at the end of her afternoon in midtown. She didn't turn to see me waiting until her bus came. Neither of us could know that the three-week press junket would become eight months in West Berlin.

22

"I wondered when you would get here." I blocked the doorway, speaking slowly, as if the tall young man may not speak English. In my outrage at having been stood up at Tempelhof Airport, I'd forgotten I was speaking to my interpreter.

"If you want to be mad at me, let me come in." He strode past me, folded his arms across his chest, stared me down and said in perfect English, "You! You were not where you were supposed to be."

It was hard to know if he could seriously be lying into my eyes. I was instantly attracted to the pale face, the high cheek bones, and even his belligerence. I replied, overly enunciating, as if English was *my* second language.

"This is unacceptable, totally unacceptable. I am not staying here."

I'd had two hours to plan my escape from this austere *pension*. I could see the legendary Hotel Kempinski from my window, and was more and more determined to be there, as soon as the missing guide from the Press Office arrived.

Having established his *correctness*, my interpreter-guide became matter-of-fact, now free to speak quietly into the phone and arranging, in a matter of minutes, my transfer to the lobby of the Hotel Kempinski. I'd never expected to get the upgrade. I was playing with the hollow-cheeked German who had an uncanny resemblance to

Oscar Werner, the "Jules" of *Jules and Jim*, a film that had transfixed "New Wave" audiences in recent months. I'd seen it twice in a dress rehearsal for the life I might create if only I could get far enough away from the city, which belonged to my mother. She *was* New York because I had given it to this woman, docile and depressed or raging full steam ahead.

"I'll wait for you in the dining hall." Eckart's accent was stronger now that we were in the Kempinski lobby. His shoulders held back, his gaze steady as he sized up his charge and her luggage. Before I could demand anything more, he turned and walked away with his hands clasped behind him, the way Collin could instantly become Prince Philip, a few years ago in Montreal.

From the moment I demanded the transfer to the Kempinski, I volleyed with Eckart. Whether we visited the Wall, where he somberly pointed out the *Vopo*s at rest with their machine guns slung casually across their shoulders or visited a Catholic Church whose courtyard was ringed in a symbolic barbed wire memorial, Eckart studied my reactions, awaiting another battle, or at least an ambush.

As we left the reconstructed Catholic Church, I pulled off my scarf and stared past the barbed wire memorial fence, to the abstract metal sculpture dedicated to millions of Hitler's victims. Suddenly I wanted to be alone, didn't want to hear more of the Press Office patter, which he delivered perfectly. I was transfixed by the fence, never having been so close to rusted barbs.

"You're Catholic! That's it, Catholic, right?" Eckart exclaimed with excitement and relief.

"Why should I be Catholic?" I looked at him too intensely.

"Catholic women cover their heads. You're so dark. I was sure you are Italian."

"Do you want me to be Italian?" I was stunned to be flirting with him, in the shadow of the symbolic barbed wire, but flirting just the same.

"I think I have been speaking too much, maybe even speaking against Jews. Did I say such things yesterday?" He was addressing the overcast sky.

If I'd told the truth, I'd have said, "Yes... you did and it shocked me... and I don't know where you really stand." But in those moments I was more taken with his appeal than with the truth and so used to being divided, that I could look into his large gray eyes and say, "I don't remember. No. I don't think so."

For the next few days, we continued my official tour, had a driver take us through West Berlin and had lunches in the best restaurants. The snowy linens were heavier than any I'd seen in New York; the middle-aged waiters made me wonder where they'd been twenty years before. When they bowed deferentially, as we made our way to the table, it seemed ludicrous that we, the kids, should be served by them. We were penniless and without any real accomplishment. We sat opposite one another at these regal meals as if we were entitled, not the accidental invitees. I was the stand-in for Mayor Daley, and Eckart was the student guide who ironed his shirts at midnight.

We had enough of the player to carry it off, ordering delicacies as if we always had such choices. He patiently explained the difference between a Mosel and a Rhine wine and described how Germans wait for the white asparagus to celebrate spring and how the spears were to be eaten with new potatoes and a slice of *schinken*. This information was neutral, even charming to me and kept us off chancier topics.

I was in alien territory and gave into the *otherness*, even to the danger of flirtation. Was I so spent from the years of filling in for my father's escape that I had nothing to lose? Did the young interpreter increase the distance between me and my mother so that I felt more at ease with the ambivalent German than I could ever feel in New York? Or had those Little Red School House days in the Village signed me up for world peace and the lamb lying down with the lion? Years later I will be astonished at how, despite my friends' tacit and not so tacit horror, I had taken the job with *Twen* and the press junket to a bisected, turbulent Berlin.

At another lunch, I listened raptly to a description of his privileged childhood cut short by Hitler's "police action" in Poland, which drafted his father into the reservist army and where in the woods, Polish cadets, uninformed of the surrender, shot his father Heinz in his tank. Eckart made sure I understood that his father had not been a Nazi, but was forced to sign up because Hitler cleverly used the reservists, who came from the dueling societies, to attack the Poles. Then abruptly, he interrupted his own story, raised his hand for the waiter, and asked me,

"You will have dessert? The *lingonberries* are so good with *schlagsahne*..."

After he gave the dessert order, after the break he needed, he resumed his account. In a few days Poland surrendered, and a chauffeur-driven car took his mother to his father's gravesite. The death notices of the "police action," as Hitler called the invasion were printed in the papers, edged in black, with a cross beside each one. As the war progressed, he told me, there would be no more black borders, just long lists.

As it became clear that the famed *schriftsteller* Grass was not going to cooperate easily for my interview and that the meeting would have to be renegotiated, I told myself I'd be returning to Berlin after Hamburg and Cologne—not for Eckart, but for the coveted interview.

When I called Franny to confess my attraction to Eckart, she applauded my new adventure and wasn't a bit miffed that I wouldn't be coming to Burgundy. We were still post-collegiate at heart, gliding through time and space.

That last evening, Eckart dismissed our driver and announced he would take the car to the Opera and then back to the Kempinski. Near midnight, parked in the official car, arguing over Wagner, but careful to avoid the anti-semite debate the musical genius could trigger, he brought his face as close to mine as possible, without touching my cheek.

I was puzzled and charmed by the mixed message I was getting under a street lamp in the chilly car. I studied his face in the shadows until he circled to the hotel entrance, got out, and with a touch of arch gallantry, opened my door and held out his hand. The doorman watched intently as we said goodnight and agreed to meet early in the morning for my departure to Munich. Bless the difficult, famous author I thought as I waited for the elevator. I'll soon be coming back to West Berlin.

The exotic, the unfamiliar was obvious. Our gene pools had never crossed; our fathers would have been enemies; we had nothing in common. I didn't know then how Bea had prepared me for Eckart, who, despite his foreignness, was familiar. I was used to trying to get her attention. In some deep place, I was more at ease with *less* and still years away from knowing how entangled I was with her.

My guide in Cologne was a middle-aged woman who paused hesitantly when speaking, reminding me of a tentative elementary school teacher, unsure if she can control her class. As Frau Wechsel showed me around Cologne, I decided not to stick her up with tough questions. I was confused enough about being in Germany and didn't want to expose her to the conflict that I put on each morning along with my smart navy suit, the suit that was supposed to describe me as professional and in which I could hide. Did the Press Office purposely hire these squashy, pudding-faced housewives to be guides? I had another one in Munich. She could have been wearing an apron, with her hands covered in flour, as we drove up to the entrance of Dachau, the extermination camp I felt compelled to visit. When it had been put on my tour in New York, the German Information secretary had asked if I was "sure" and I'd replied "yes," unable to imagine actually driving through the gates.

Without looking up from her clipboard, my guide handed me the official program notes for the tour of the camp and kept up a patter, a hum of information—how many visitors make the pilgrimage, how records are kept, how it was decided not to create a museum but to keep the buildings and grounds as close to how they were just twenty years before.

Having dared myself to come to the camp, I now could not bear to take it in. Although I stood under the gas jets, I'll never be able to describe the chamber: for as I looked up to the ceiling, I blocked the naked women and children beneath it . . . and stood silent where there had been screams. My guide walked purposefully towards the exit as if to give me some privacy. I stood in place, in a freeze frame, until the wave of dizziness settled and I could walk back into the sunlight. The early signs of spring that day made me shudder: the birds that had finally returned, years after Dachau's liberation, were singing in the new green as we got into the car.

When I tried to describe the camp to Eckart or others, I couldn't recall enough to tell anything more than what *Life* magazine photographs had already told. I had no details to add. I told myself that returning to the bisected city was a professional move: for the interview and not for the dashing, tentative German interpreter. It was possible for me to use the last of my German press stipend for a return ticket to West Berlin because, again, being divided, not fully present—in the doorway—was familiar, enabling me to bury my reactions to what I'd seen that morning at Dachau and, even more importantly, to what I'd imagined.

Eckart shared a fifth-floor apartment in a turn-of-the-century building with two roommates. This apartment building, on Niebuhrstrasse just off the famous Kurfürstendamm Boulevard, was opposite a bombed-out structure whose foundation was a kind of crater, filled with

Iolanthe trees like the ones in New York. West Berlin was still littered with signs of the bombings that had decimated it. The shattered brick and mortar was not as hard to witness as the limbless (not just veterans) going about their business, in sturdy and not so sturdy wheelchairs and walkers. Eckart carried my bags up a wide wooden staircase to the fifth floor, unlocked the multiple locks of the 1920s when break-ins were rampant, and led me to his once elegant, now threadbare room, overlooking the bombed-out ruin across the street, weeds entangled with concrete and a jumble of green more horrifying than comforting—a smashed city, its broken story in full view.

I can't remember being asked to stay, or my asking. I do remember feeling that if anything was explicit nothing would happen between us. It's just for a short time, I told myself. Play it out. Watch everything. You will never be here again. You'll be gone, writing up your interview back on East 70th Street before you've even learned the words for milk and eggs.

For a few weeks, we lay half the day on a mattress on the floor, side by side, not touching, talking as the sun warmed the worn parquet. Eckart had been to America, a Fulbright Exchange Student at Northwestern. It seemed he wanted me to know he'd been fascinated with a graduate student whose family was Portuguese, who welcomed him at her family picnics, where lamb was slowly turned on a spit. He emphasized that her hair was as dark as mine. I will never know if she became his real girlfriend. I was listening hard for clues, his intentions... and hang ups? How to be his type? What I didn't know then was that I was also ignoring the signs that Eckart offered *little*—which suited the implicit pact I'd made with my mother when I was suddenly good-looking that last year of high school, when she went mad: I will never have more than you've had, never be more, never leave you.

Away from New York, I was a long-distance swimmer who had breathlessly made shore but was only dimly aware of the incongruity of it all. I was living with a German *student* in a forbidden city where I'd have been one of the ones unable to leave her dachshund and her geraniums and would have been one of the taken. At that time I hadn't learned that my mother's mother was born in Berlin and came, as a two-year-old, to New Jersey. This discovery, decades later, will create yet another lens with which to adjust that time on Niebuhrstrasse, and to see how waiting for the Grass interview would create the next twenty years.

At dusk, the light in his room was mesmerizing. A glass of wine carried me through the changing hues. The azure blue in the huge window recalled a scrim behind the dancers at City Center on 55th Street. Eckart called it "your blue light" and brought our glasses to the table between the two frayed velvet armchairs facing the window. We talked into the blue light until dark, never facing each other.

One evening I nearly whispered, "I should tell you. My mother's in and out of mental hospitals."

I studied his face as he leaned forward to fill his glass, his gray eyes ever steady.

"That's no big deal. Every family has a crazy person. We have my Aunt Nora. No one understands her," implying that only he did.

"This is different. She can't be at home." The gory details could wait. It was enough to have his non-reaction, which was endearing, nearly erotic.

We continued to have lunch as the main meal but now, off the Press Office expense account, we went to neighborhood places: narrow Chinese restaurants and Serbian lunch counters where laborers mixed with clerks who walked the two blocks over from the once elegant, recovering Kurfürstendamm.

In the evening we went to Diener's, the *wurstgesheft* on Kantstrasse where local artists gathered to have their *abendsbrot*, their evening bread: liverwurst on thin black bread, the malt scent of beer filling the room. The tables were close, and the waiters handed glasses over the bent heads of customers so intent on their conversation that it seemed a beer down their shoulders would be ignored as these ardent young Berliners lectured one another. I didn't understand what they were saying, but I got the intensity and was captivated by the sheer force of both the men and the women. And besides, I was in *Jules and Jim* and not the war films that would have sent me flying back to New York. I was editing so I could have this time. Like so many lovers who should have remained friends, talk was our bridge. When we finally made love we held one another, wordlessly. Now if only for the summer, I had a German boyfriend and the images, the scents, the sounds of West Berlin would become indelible. With my hand in his, Eckart showed me his adopted city. He took my hand the way he'd guided me around that first week, in charge, paternal.

As summer in Berlin went on, there was hardly ever a hot day, instead the sky was milky and heavy with clouds. The Berliners,

Eckart said, liked to remind themselves that the poet Heinrich Heine described summer as "Berlin's Green Winter." I will discover Heine was the only poet my Grandma Tess had memorized as a girl in Vienna.

Eckart continued to work for the Press Office. I spent mornings with my journal. Afternoons were for exploring the neighborhood. I took a string bag from the kitchen, where his roommate's dirty plates were piled on worn marble counters and returned in time to improvise supper. But I refused to clean up Siegfried and Helmut's mess and instead, with perfected tunnel vision, handled our food like a lab technician, separating our dishes from theirs, keeping food tightly wrapped and tucked into our corner of the refrigerator.

A California commune we were not. No cheerful gatherings at the table, shared tasks, stories, or casseroles. The two men slouched silently down the long hall leading to the kitchen, mumbling a greeting but backing off when they saw one of us already at the chopping block. Eckart told me not to use garlic or, if I must, to shut the kitchen door so the odor wouldn't drift into the apartment. When I reminded him it was *aroma,* he elaborated on the instruction, saying that garlic in Germany was associated with immigrants from the East, garlic-chewing Jews. I never found out if that was generally believed or his own private anti-semitic family folklore.

It made me queasy to face his crazy ideas about Jews so I reminded myself this was a fling. I was taking a break. It was 1964 and transatlantic calls were too costly for even my mother to make. My connection to the kitchen, to the apartment in general, was temporary. This was a campsite I would never see again and could, defiantly, leave as littered as I'd found it.

Finally, more than a month after our original appointment, the award-winning writer had agreed. We were to have the interview at his house. Eckart resumed his official role and delivered me to Günter Grass's doorstep, leaving me to do my job. Frau Grass led the way upstairs to his study, opened the door and motioned for me to enter. Then she closed the door, a woman accustomed to giving her husband his stage, his privacy. There was no one in the room. I took a seat.

Felt slippers appeared first at the top of the spiral staircase, as the most celebrated writer in Europe began his descent from the loft.

"So! Ah so! Here is the American reporter."

He stared intently, glasses on the bridge of his prominent nose, as he extended his hand, which was rough, nearly chapped. He sighed, not with displeasure but with *ennui* and gestured towards the chair facing his desk, bringing me closer.

I'd waited so many weeks for this meeting that I was more prepared than for the interviews I'd done for *Twen* with writers (Philip Roth and others) at The Algonquin Hotel on 44th Street. But I was not on home ground. It won't be the Madison Avenue bus I'll take back to my apartment. I was sweating through my silk blouse and glad for the jacket that covered it.

"What is it you've come for?" The *auteur provocateur* asked, as he arranged his crotch in the corduroy slacks and crossed his legs, letting his slippers slide to the carpet. I was tempted to blurt out "an intimate portrait" but instead became the rapt reporter asking for reactions to his latest prize. Just four years after graduation, how did I have the audacity to be doing what I was doing? Because I had spent four years at a college that gave me permission to sit across from famous scholars and writers and to believe that my queries were as valid as anyone else's. If I could flirt with Joseph Campbell as I presented a plan for my senior paper, I could sit across from this prize-winner without apology; far from New York and tucked, albeit provisionally, into Niebuhrstrasse, I was feeling my power in totally new ways. As always, the far-from-New York part was the keystone to feeling safer.

Grass's black eyes locked with mine as he dismissed my questions. The double message was that although my questions were irrelevant this afternoon, surely we will have to meet again to get anything substantial for my story. He ushered me to the door, his hand firmly on my elbow.

"We will see once more. You will telephone."

Eckart couldn't help himself. He asked for a description of everything. Siegfried and Helmut want to know how it went, he explained. The novelist was a celebrity in the bisected city, and my meeting with him, as far as they could see, was nearly historic.

I edited the afternoon and deflected Eckart's innuendo about the author's notable reputation as a womanizer. I was surprised that Eckart even cared if there was more than reportage in the meeting. Until then, there was no signal that I mattered, one way or the other.

Just when I decided to spend the rest of the summer on the mattress on the parquet floor, Eckart announced it would be a good idea for me to move to a pension. He didn't look at me as he blurted out the reasons for us to live separately. He didn't want to lead me on, he mumbled. Only a poor graduate student, he needed to finish his work, to concentrate. It seemed our lovemaking had only been hesitant coupling, a kind of laboratory. With a twinge of hurt pride, I was free to go, to move a few blocks away to the Kurfürstendamm, the grand boulevard that still showed its bones of purposeful splendor. Intentionally or not, he'd set me free. Moving out would remove the conflict that had been stirring since I'd been meeting with Grass for coffee. Now the prized writer would not be walking me back to the lobby of Niebuhrstrasse number One, to the *student* he repeatedly insisted wasn't enough for me.

Even with his cap pulled down across his forehead, Grass was always recognized, all eyes following his bandy-legged gait as he led me towards a table, his hand on my waist. One evening at a Kurfürstendamm café, he interrupted his discourse on the stagnation of European postwar writers to take my hand, to examine it. As he turned my palm up and traced the life line, he proclaimed, "This is a wonderful hand, beautiful and strong. You will do much with your life ... of course, if you don't follow too much that *Deutsche student* ..." He never missed a chance to describe Eckart as a student, instead of as the part-time student who also had a job and could soon be finished with his studies. I didn't connect these dots with what Philip had observed on East 70th Street when he'd asked if I intended to "do something." Not having gone to graduate school but already having some magazine bylines, it seemed I was doing something, albeit without a plan. My mother's swings between catatonia and manic explosions might have made me pursue an intentional life, a safe course—a sheltering marriage, a teaching degree. But instead, I was impersonating a wild girl, whirling, twirling, even daring—unable to admit how much in need of rescue I was.

Having been baffled by my attachment to Eckart, Grass was delighted to hear I'd moved to a pension close to the café where we usually met for coffee in late afternoon. I was no longer the inquiring reporter. Grass was the writer/director of the movie we were making. He described all the details of his days except his arrangement with his wife. We sat outdoors even as the air chilled and others moved quickly inside. He enjoyed the warmth of the slivovitz running down his throat, seeing his breath in the air, his piercing dark eyes as piercing as mine.

In those weeks, he kept offering to give me an apartment where I could have a *salon*. A *salon*? Did he know a Greenwich Village *geisha* when he met one? He took up this fantasy whenever we met for schnapps... ensconced in his imagined apartment, I would give Sunday afternoon salons attended by his fascinating colleagues. I would dazzle his friends, implying that a life with the *student* will never give me the stage I deserved. I was once more in the tangled web of writers and erotica, only this time the Village kid, far from Washington Square, was surprisingly more at ease, with the author winning all the prizes. (His Nobel will come twenty years later.)

Because attraction is often the mirror lovers hold up—giving us our best selves—I was now more and more attracted to this man, whose first entrance had been disarming but not seductive as he shuffled across his Persian carpet in slippers.

I wondered how he knew Sunday afternoons made me feel adrift and lonely ever since childhood and how had he come up with the salon image? Did he know more about my zest for drama than I did then? Had he inadvertently been paying attention?

One late afternoon I called to confirm our coffee date. "Good! It is good you are calling me now! Do you know what I am, in this very moment, doing?" He rolled on before I could reply.

"I am just now drawing a beautiful fish. I brought him from the market today. First I must draw him, then I will flour him, and then cook him and, yes, I will eat him!"

He was triumphant, brimming with his creation of a life that intrigued, fed him and allowed him to roam at will.

"And when I am finished, I will come to visit you!"

That evening my landlady, Frau Schnabel, led him down the hall to my *Berlinerzimmer*. He'd brought along his favorite clear apple brandy, produced two thimble glasses from a chamois pouch and poured the *schnaps*. Those afternoons in cafes had been intense and graceful, a minuet. The man who'd noticed the details, and made me feel *seen* was was not the one pouring the *schnaps*.

In the next few days, when I made it clear that more talk was all I wanted, he stopped calling. But not before he warned that life with Eckart would be only mediocre, pale in comparison to the imaginary salon he'd offered.

Eckart continued to be the reluctant boyfriend. It was finally tiresome even for a girl given to magical thinking. I announced I was returning to New York. He could follow or not. For a few days he insisted on staying in West Berlin. But as soon as I accepted his refusal, Eckart had a ticket to arrive two days after I did. We would, he assured me, be traveling like the royal family on different planes. Not a bad allusion for a penniless *student*.

23

"Bea is in Bellevue." My father's alliteration will not be lost on me when I replay my homecoming tape from Berlin. *Replay* is how I've learned to deal with what's going on with my mother because during the actual event I was absent, *in the doorway,* just as I'd been on 10ᵗʰ Street, Waverly Place, Bleecker Street, North Hollywood, Charlton Street, West End Avenue, and finally 83ʳᵈ Street. He couldn't hold back the details until after I'd found my luggage. "She's where? Bellevue?" Bea had made the big time, no more little Westchester loony bins. Now she was certifiably crazy in Manhattan.

Summer had come to New York the usual way, on the heels of May. The ride into the city could have been taking us towards Calcutta as my father tersely reported that although my mother had held up the past few months, she'd gone wild in her lobby a few days ago, the police had been called, and now she was locked up. He had no plans to visit.

Was I relieved she'd been in Bellevue for just a few days or shaken that it had happened at all? As always her escapades sent me spinning, the storyline broken, the narrator unreliable, the punchline missing.

The next morning I walked down the lime green corridor which would lead to my mother. The floor nurse simultaneously murmured directions to the locked ward, took a call, and continued filling out a form. I hoped it wasn't a requisition for some poor patient's meds, the cocktails which could be lethal even if given in prescribed amounts. I was shivering, although the hospital air-conditioning was more of a gesture than a solution. Jet lag, I reassured myself, scanning the letters on the doors. Disinfectant fumes rose from the cracked linoleum. Would it be like those times at Pinewood after shock treatments? When her gaze made me feel I was invisible or a speck on her horizon.

Too easily, I pushed open a door that should have been locked and entered a room the size of my high school gym, terrified that I wouldn't find my mother in this crowd, terrified that I would. Patients were sitting abjectly on folding chairs or rocking back and forth precariously or leaning against the green walls, as if they were waiting for buses or an announcement. They were all women and all wearing hospital gowns over night clothes. My eyes were adjusting to the swarm of faces, when suddenly the unwashed harpy, swaying in front of me was my mother; her hospital gown hanging off a bare shoulder, her raspy Thorazine damaged voice crying out, "You! Get me out of here!" Her nails clutched my arm just above my wrist, where they always dug in. She hadn't seen me in more than eight months.

Turning to a sedated, older woman, coming too close to the woman's ashen face, she croaked, picking up the volume as she shouted out,

"That twerp! Hiding in Germany... with the Nazis!" Her eyes sparkled.

I moved quickly away to search the crowd for someone official. After a few false starts to get an orderly's attention, I found a young Chinese doctor carrying a clipboard. Surely he could help me help her. He motioned to the edge of the room, away from the women who were crying, giggling, sulking, and sniffling without tissues at hand. My mother spotted us, and wobbled over to peer over his clipboard. He motioned again for her to stand aside, to give us privacy as if we're stepping into his invisible office. What are these hand gestures for? I still hadn't heard a word from him. When I began my questions, which I hoped would lead to her release back to Pinewood, he nodded, smiling broadly.

"What happened to my mother? Why is she here?" I was over enunciating the way you do with the hard of hearing. The doctor smiled again, fingering his stethoscope as nervously as some men finger their ties. He glanced at his clipboard, as if the answer was somewhere close at hand. Reading his badge, I persevered.

"Dr Chen, can you tell me..."

"Ah, ah. English. No speak English."

By the end of the day, my mother's Chinese psychiatrist at Bellevue, who spoke no English, arranged for her transfer back to our familiar Westchester homestead, Pinewood Sanatorium. I was too numb to contemplate what might have happened to her had I stayed longer in West Berlin.

"I sailed on *The Liberté*! You should have met me then!" My mother tossed the line over her shoulder to Eckart, who stood with his hands behind his back: Prince Philip in the director's office at Pinewood.

Although I had set up this appointment, I was mortified that Eckart was meeting my mother, for the first time, in this place. Manic agitation propelled her from the desk, where she slammed her hand down for emphasis. Despite my getting her out of Bellevue, she'd barely looked at me. My attempt at a hello hug had been shrugged off and today, even her cheek was not offered.

"Did you enjoy the voyage on the French ship, Mrs. Gravenson?" Eckart leaned forward from the waist, holding his head to one side, as if he was examining a specimen at The American Museum of Natural History. She seemed taken by his formality and stopped pacing to consider the question, while the director, Dr. Wilber, watched the match.

"Enjoy? That's a roll in the hay . . . to enjoy!" My mother, who only referred to sex (and never to lovemaking) when she was high, paused for reaction. When Eckart looked unflinchingly into her eyes, she pulled herself together.

"Of course, the voyage was superb, elegant. As expected." She'd become Mary Astor again, a class act.

I watched with horror and disbelief as my mother flirted with my boyfriend who'd arrived in New York two days before. At my insistence, we'd rushed up to Pinewood so my mother could meet the person who'd kept me so far away. I'd been told she was in a calmer mood, that a meeting was possible. I must have wanted to test Eckart.

"Let me tell you ,. . ." her voice was guttural, her eyes narrowed," there's money to be made." She was nodding for emphasis. "Who the hell are you? Kidnapping my girl!" She clasped her heaving bosom as if she were overcome with the discovery that I was still her daughter, not yet disowned, not yet the wrong baby.

We drove back to Manhattan in my father's Buick. Like other summers, dusty green foliage lined the parkway. And even though this trip had become routine, I was breathless in the front seat, as winded as if I'd raced up the driveway.

"She did not trouble me. Not a bit." Eckart's eyes were on the road, his hand covering mine. I felt the warmth of his hand and gave in to the weight of it as much as I did when his body covered mine. And let out my breath.

My father caved in and gave Eckart a summer job at his ad agency, probably hoping it would seal the deal of my non-courtship. Ted was relieved to find out when we'd met a few months before in Genoa that my boyfriend was from *West* not *East* Germany. As we'd floated on our backs in the hotel pool, I'd heard him sigh as if to say ... if it has to be a German, please let it be one from the West.

How hard it was for Eckart to be working for my father was lost on me. I was focused on the shame and trouble my mother made, blind to the obvious risk of subjecting my beloved to the snares of being employed by his future father-in- law even though marriage had still never come up.

Inexplicably, I continued to be employed by *Twen* and didn't need to return to a staff job, at least not for the summer. We were offered a house-sitting on upper Central Park West, where we would be astonished by the gray and soiled sheets left in the toddler's crib. We closed the door to that room and never opened it again. Appalled, we agreed that such a crib could never exist in our imaginary house.

As summer drew to a close, Eckart's departure became the issue. I knew where I would be at the end of the month—at home in New

York. His whereabouts were less compelling now that, back in my real life, I could admit defeat and could let him go.

On a September evening, as we were dressing to go downtown to my father and Clarice's place, Eckart joined me in front of the steamy bathroom mirror. Knotting his tie, he watched as I leaned forward to apply mascara with my usual devotion. Before I had traced each lash, he announced with studied casualness,

"Now, now that you can get ready in time . . . we may as well get married." Then checked his watch, straightened his tie and grinned at me in the mirror.

Like so many men, who think they are the gift, he had no other offering. I was too surprised, in the moment, to even notice that he didn't take me in his arms, didn't touch me at all. Even if I longed for more to hold and remember, I was getting what I thought I wanted. I had come this far with him on so little, accustomed and comfortable with less rather than more. I smiled at him in the mirror, wordlessly agreeing to his non-proposal. I was proving my father wrong: a man who knew all about Bea would marry me.

We splurged on a taxi downtown and told my father and Clarice before the wine was poured. Ted beamed as broadly as when he landed an account. Clarice beckoned me to her closet, to display the blue satin sheath she'd been planning to wear more than once.

"We're so excited. We've been hoping." She smoothed the satin over her hips as she showed it off in the mirror. Her eyes matched the sheath, and her Revlon mouth glistened. She smiled at me, but the powdered face was wrong and the high shrill voice repelled me. I was in the mirror with the wrong woman.

"We'll go together! I'll shop with you, and we'll find just the right dress!" She turned to hang up her gown without a word from me.

My stepmother didn't deserve this, but I was still hoping for my crazy mother to reappear as a regular Mom, if only for a few days, a few hours, to walk me down the aisle with my father, whom she hadn't seen in five years unless you counted her last explosive, straitjacketed exit from his office.

We left the Central Park West apartment and took one on West 81st opposite The American Museum of Natural History. The ceilings were high and the view beyond the Planetarium, to the east side, was more than we'd hoped for, although the park across the street would soon be home to drug dealing and referred to as "Needle Park." Months later, a citywide blackout made us face the dangers. After we'd moved from that apartment, Eckart admitted that he'd watched me waiting at the bus stop each morning, waiting to see me safely inside, before leaving the window. This and his taking my hand when we stepped off a curb will come back even when he's no longer my *safe* person. Protection would take the place of ardent love making, and would allow me to marry.

It was fall, and my mother was still locked away in Pinewood. We planned to be married in January. Just days before the wedding Leonard called. In familiar, hushed tones, he determined that he had the right number and could he drop by for a visit? I was several years from that time on Hydra, and about to marry the elusive German. I told him we were fixing up our apartment without mentioning the wedding. An hour later, I heard a tap on our door.

"Of course, there you are," Leonard whispered, holding a large bouquet of wildflowers. He'd found Queen Anne's lace and Black-Eyed Susans on the Upper West Side, in December. "For you," he intoned solemnly, grinning in delight at his own gallantry.

Eckart came forward to be introduced, bowing ever so slightly from the waist. Both young men took each other in. Sensing the visit would be brief, I went to the kitchen to plunge the bouquet into a vase, without removing its paper or trimming its stems. Leaning against the counter, I closed my eyes—to stop the film, to steady myself. I didn't want to miss a minute of this short clip but also didn't want to be tempted back to the island, to the blue and white palette of Greece, to Leonard's mysterious profile, to poetry—to life as art.

The two of them had jumped eagerly into the Vietnam debate, which Eckart had introduced. On firm ground now, he dominated the conversation, leaving the poet behind. When Leonard stood up to leave, he offered his hand to Eckart who was now at ease, no longer deferential.

"I'm walking Leonard to the elevator," I called out, taking his coat from the hall closet.

"This will be splendid," Leonard murmured, holding me against his narrow chest, as he had on Hydra's quay, as we waited for the elevator. The Rabbi Poet smiled a blessing, as the door slid shut, leaving me to wonder if it was my life with Eckart or just the wedding that would be splendid. I was relieved Leonard hadn't stayed for the evening, for I was marrying Eckart who I've decided, against the evidence, was steady and reliable because he was unperturbed by my mother, who continued to invade my dreams . . . Bea flying into a crowd of well-wishers at our ceremony, half-dressed, in full throttle or me in a meadow, not able to see clearly (a myopic's terror) to know if the animal stalking me is a large dog or a mountain lion. These dreams must have been payment for choosing the date, which will guarantee her still in Pinewood, not part of the party.

When we sent word to the German Information Center that we would marry in December, they congratulated us and added that Eckart's assignment had not been for life. I could imagine the chuckles overlooking Park Avenue. What was more of a surprise was Grass responding to the news with "Dear Linda, for you and Eckart the best for the first seven years of your marriage. After the first seven luck, always luck." He added that he'd be in New York in February and could be reached at Harcourt. Although he suggested I write to him I couldn't risk it. I would be just a month into my marriage with the German *student* he'd dismissed, whom I'd become more involved with while waiting for the much postponed interview. If not for Grass, Eckhart would've remained a mystery instead of becoming a life choice.

The search for a veil took me to 38th Street between Sixth and Seventh Avenues. The storefront windows were enticing and belied the tumult inside, where silk roses tumbled against spools of satin ribbon and piles of tulle lay against each other, like so many Degas girls in repose. I threw myself upon the mercy of the saleswomen—to guide me around, to stand in for the missing mother.

As I pored through layers of silk and organza, graduation from high school and college raced across the screen. So even as I longed for her to be with me, even to be arguing like other mothers and daughters, I had to admit it was a relief that she was still in Pinewood and would remain there when we celebrated.

My father was so elated by our news that he impulsively arranged a tour of the Plaza's White and Gold Room, but when costs became clear he reneged. I was relieved, for how could I have had such an opulent affair and break my still unconscious pledge never to have more than Bea? Instead of dinner at the Plaza, we would have an after-dinner dance at the Fifth Avenue Hotel, just a block from my childhood 10th Street. Gail had come to my rescue by planning an evening that could be seen as original, not penny-pinching. Although she'd moved to D.C., she orchestrated the plans and kept emphasizing that we were Village Kids (she'd played on the East side of the Arch when I was playing on the West) who always did better Downtown. She framed the compromise, accentuating the positive—something she had a knack for and that I needed then and would need in years to come.

We were married on a bright, frigid January morning in the chapel of the Unitarian Church on Park and 35th Street. This minister had welcomed us when every rabbi I'd called discouraged the match. I don't remember why my father did not walk me down the chapel's short aisle. Instead, he and Clarice and our witnesses, Henry and Sheila, stood with us before the minister. For an instant, I imagined my mother taking her place beside my father, wearing the same hat she'd worn that sultry June afternoon at Sarah Lawrence.

A transit strike had paralyzed the city, and even limos were unavailable. My father drove the Buick around in sub-freezing weather to pick up our elderly relatives, unable to get a cab. But never mind—the mood was festive as we stood on the receiving line and smiled at people clearly examining the groom... a German, but at least tall and good looking, not too blond. What could you expect when you sent her to that Commie school in the Village where that one-world idea could only bring *trouble.* They didn't know then that the diffident German will find a way to blend in by referring to *Europe* when he means Germany.

Totally assimilated and non-observant, my relatives still held dear the totems of a world lost while they were safe, here, on the other side. They expected ritual and instead were given a dance, without dinner. It could have been worse, they told my father. She could have found a Negro. A few years later, I will wonder if Eckart's unease, so clear in the photographs, was a foreign groom's natural hesitancy, or the wariness of a creature, cornered—even if a few of the photos do show him smiling at his bride, who looks adoringly up at him.

When the guests had left and we were back upstairs in our chilly, threadbare room, its 1929 splendor long gone, my new husband stuffed every towel he could against the old windows. Spent, we fell asleep, entwined for warmth. We didn't have a honeymoon or even a little trip out of town. It must have been about money and time and the fact that we'd been living together off and on for a year and a half. I do remember the stab of disappointment and, even more, the vow to keep that to myself.

We saw the walk-up in Brooklyn Heights after work, with a whizzing, asthmatic managing agent who only showed apartments in the evening, although the electricity was disconnected. A candle, provided by the agent, created shadows on the walls as we glimpsed a peek-a-boo view of the Harbor and said we'd take it. It would turn out that leaving Manhattan would be a much bigger deal than either of us could anticipate. My fear of subways was submerged in the service of getting this terrific little place—rent controlled, two bright rooms with an air shaft kitchen, overlooking the Plymouth Church where Harriet Beecher Stowe had spoken so eloquently. On the fourth floor, on Orange Street, we squabbled and made up—a couple in turmoil not marital bliss. If my mother sensed these were turbulent times for us, she didn't ration her emergency calls.

Somehow we managed to create a working-couple life, living in our pleasant three-room apartment and commuting to work in Manhattan. We even took the subway together. I had my German Shepherd to guide me through the throngs I finally confessed to fearing, although I barely mentioned the jaundiced face I'd looked into when I swung my bag and sent the man flying down the steps of the urine-smelling subway stairwell. Instead of owning the terror of that day, I emphasized Bea's terror of crowds and being underground. Her avoidance of the subway started after my grandfather's heart attack when I was four.

My father's insistence to stay home with me when babysitters were available had become another chapter in the mystery stories my parents created for themselves. I have no memory of ever taking the subway with my mother.

I blamed my gloomy moods on Bea's intrusions or the worry that came when she didn't surface. Where was she wandering now? What was she up to? Eckart, gloomy, in his own way, was harder to track. Were his moods due to the war and the lost father, whose body lay in Poland? Was his market research job so numbing? Especially for a man who had joked about becoming Chancellor of West Germany. How to explain why he often disappeared into remoteness after we'd made love, as if to say, this hasn't happened, you've imagined it. I was still murmuring "I love you" before, during or after as he remained silent. Yet he was still my guide, taking my hand when we crossed the street, and most importantly, making sure Bea knew who was boss.

Months after we married, we had a non-honeymoon in St. Martin. While I sat beneath a banyan tree, Eckart photographed teenage black boys thrashing gleefully in the turquoise water. I was unable to get his attention until he'd captured the high spirits, the glistening bodies. In 1968 our troubles were mysterious, yet after three years of marriage, we planned a baby. A baby would make Eckart safe from the draft and keep me safer from Bea than with him in Vietnam.

24

Years later, Nico, who'd just turned seven, when the shades are up and the light is everywhere, was sent under the table by one of Bea's explosions. The table is beside the Christmas tree trimmed with wooden ornaments he loved, given by the German grandma he will remember fondly. He crouched there, for more time than I want to recall, until we heard the slamming of the front door.

"Now we must stop!" Bea hissed, as if this were a performance we'd all agreed to. Eckart dropped his briefcase, saw his son under the table, and spread his arms for him. As he hoisted Nico against his overcoat, he simultaneously announced he was calling Bea's cab. I was astonished to see her comply, make a trip to the bathroom, and return with newly applied lipstick for the trip home. She didn't say another word as she moved to the vestibule and stoop. The visiting Granny awaiting her cab is what the neighbors would see.

Sitting on the edge of Nico's bed, I brushed his bangs aside, "Grandma wasn't mad at you. She's sometimes angry but never with you. Try to remember that, sweetheart." He listened politely, shrugged, and turned to the wall. I bent to kiss him and got the salty scent of his hair. As I went down the long staircase, I was burning with rage at her, at our bad luck for her to be crazy, and at myself for not getting better, faster. I hadn't known where to draw the line because that line, those boundaries, eluded me, but now I had to protect my child by getting out of this, by being able to be his mother outside, and off the block. Just as I'd felt panic in my muscles, closing my throat these years, I felt this urgency as if it had taken up residence in my body. I was running out of time.

The next morning I called Bea to tell her that unless she stayed on the prescribed lithium, which she had been skipping, she wouldn't be seeing her grandson. My little boy under the table had drawn the line. Years later, Nico, who has become Nick at college, will tell me he knew that day that she'd never be like other grandmas, and yet in his infinite sweetness he never held back greeting her with a kiss and kept reciting his Little League triumphs if she might stop to listen.

I began a search for a way out that wasn't all talk. I consulted a homeopathic MD, an Indian in Gucci loafers, who told me that all my symptoms were classic low thyroid issues, and that he could not begin treatment until I was off the Valium I'd been taking under Mallman's guidance. He was adamant, but I left his office unable to agree to give up the drug, which as it would turn out, had been having a paradoxical effect, especially in long-term use. For months, I deliberated between complying with the homeopath's requirement or continuing my daily Valium, which unbeknownst to me was keeping me anxious.

Once more, Mexico would provide a bandage if not a cure: we were visiting my parents in San Miguel when an excursion to the Pacific Coast, to Manzanillo, was an unexpected treat. The ocean created its rhythmic hum, the birds their song, and the lavenders and oranges at dawn and dusk were so saturated they seemed newly minted. I'd stopped expecting *setting* to magically bring Eckart closer. I would walk this beach myself.

On the third day I stopped at the water's edge and said out-loud, "I'm not taking anymore Valium. I'm going back to Cherian." And let myself slide into the swirling foam.

I began taking Cherian's thyroid and remedies at the same time as I began treatment with Carl Rand, a cognitive behavioral therapist, so we would never know just what got me better. Although some psychotropic drugs were being used for agoraphobia, my mother's misadventures with Thorazine and other psychotropic cocktails had created another phobia. In a well-designed, scientific experiment, my homeopathic treatment with Dr. Cherian would not have coincided with cognitive behavioral therapy, but as was true of nearly everything that had happened, mystery would prevail, including Eckart's mystery.

I had to take a car service to Carl Rand's brownstone in Park Slope. It was 1978, and the Slope was years from becoming a literary hotspot. As I walked up the stoop, I heard the deep, thunderous barking of a major dog. The vestibule was as shadowed as the House of Usher. If I weren't nearly breathless, I'd have enjoyed the irony: dimly lit as metaphor? Could I be enlightened in such gloom?

Carl Rand opened the office door and offered a damp palm. As the barking continued, he led me to an arm chair opposite his. He managed something close to a smile. The parlor was nearly as dim as the hallway, and it took a few moments to get adjusted to the light, to make out his shining bald head, his clasped hands that hid bitten nails.

"Is there a dog downstairs?" I needed to know if it was leashed or could bound up the stairwell and crash into the office. He assured me his well-trained Akita was behind a gate and would calm down now that we were settled. If I wasn't so rattled, I might have asked if the thunderous barks were a recording, part of the treatment plan, part of learning to desensitize. If he could train this beast, could he show me how to tame the demons who'd taken me away, as surely as if I'd been kidnapped?

I will soon learn that as a CBT (behaviorist) Carl believed with all his heart that thoughts control our emotions and that we can take back the control we've given up, that we can override phobias just as they have ridden us. A magical tool that even I, a doubter, could use?

His first instruction will turn out to be the most powerful in his arsenal, "Head straight into a panic attack, instead of avoiding it. It takes the body forty-five minutes to replace adrenaline. The attacks can't go on forever, and they can't kill you."

All the way home, in the cab, I repeated his promise and his parting shot, "Remember they're only time-limited!" as the Akita had barked me out.

On our next meeting he proposed that if I stayed in what scared me and didn't abort it or flee, I'd literally be desensitizing to that particular fear. Although he believed my terror, he wasn't interested in the gory details, didn't want me to rehearse them as I had with Mallman, didn't want me to examine or have me create the metaphors. He looked at me steadily and said with emphasis on every word,

"I want you to let your mind change the subject so your nervous system can calm down."

Here would be slow, painstaking work that seemed like voodoo. Instead of peeling the Freudian onion, I was told to cut it in half, inhale the sharp vapors, and wait for my eyes to adjust—which they will because I'm basically healthy (Carl insists), basically *resilient* not *basically neurotic* as Freud declared; an observation that had escaped me during those ambulance years, an observation that would have served me well and perhaps kept me from my own emergency years. *Basically healthy* would separate me from Bea, a separation I was unable to imagine until now. Nico, at seven, cowering under the table, would be my talisman for this journey. The light was up.

After all this time, I had someone telling me I won't be like this forever, who was as intent on reassurance as I was on doubting the outcome. Wasn't I Bea's daughter? And hadn't her other siblings (4 out of 6) been not "okay"? How much was chemistry and how much was her story? How much was her? How was I wired? Wasn't my fate hinged with hers?

I didn't know then that I was moving from blaming her to cursing fate, hers and mine, that hearing I was the wrong baby was better than being no one's baby and so, like so many others, I would take it, whatever *it* was, and that if not for agoraphobia, I'd have created another illness, to keep me glued to Bea and Eckart—albeit yearning to be free. For *yearning* was what I'd taken away from those Village days.

I also didn't know that years down the road, I would see her as more tragic than malevolent—a victim. And that I'd made choices even when it seemed I was on automatic pilot. I had years to go to get out of the blaming business.

Carl repeatedly pointed out that Bea could never do the exercises, accept a teacher, and stick to the rules that would lead me out. When I began to see how I could do this and how she couldn't, I had to admit to what I'd been denying for years: my mother was as sick as if she had cancer. It was the chemistry talking, killing with words and sometimes rough hands. The other mother was not a mirage. She had been there *before* and left her mark, which had kept me enthralled, unable to disentangle the knot of us, which now included Eckart.

Carl's job was to break down the fear until it came in manageable bites, not the wave that engulfed. When he needed to observe what happened to me on the street, he proposed that he walk behind me as I navigated the four blocks back to his stoop.

"You'll be right behind me?" I was incredulous and ashamed at how relieved I was to hear he'd be shadowing me.

"Right behind you, but I won't talk to you and you won't look back at me." He wasn't smiling but he was telling me he'd have my back.

The first block brought the heave of nausea, the second the wave of dizziness in open space, but on the third block I was able to bring up "it can't kill you" like a banner. I slowed down, breathing deeply. Tears were blurring my vision as I rounded the corner, still not looking over my shoulder. As soon as we were back in the office he took the helm.

"I'm not interested in how you *felt* doing this. I'm interested in what you *did*." His voice was nearly a whisper, as if we were collaborators.

"From now on, tell me what you *did* each week. We're not going to rehearse the failures, we're going forward." And with that, he stood and ushered me to the door, one deep howl rising from the Akita.

Each time I returned to Second Place with my new homework assignment: to practice focusing on the horizon, as I walked around the block or to Court Street to choose fruit and veggies, and to choose each day whether to be frozen or to walk back into my life.

Carl wasn't interested in my childhood habit of standing breathless in the doorway, watching for my mother's signals. It may have served me then to be wary, watchful, one step ahead of her, looking in but not present. It was just that impulse he was aiming to change.

"We're going to get you breathing again." He announced as if proposing a trip to the Amazon. "You hold your breath regularly. And that leads to hyperventilating, which leads into a panic attack." He picked up the paper bag he'd had at the ready next to his chair. "By blowing into it, you change the carbon dioxide ratio and restore normal breathing. The panic dies down. You can think straight."

Thinking straight was an intoxicating notion, as exotic as news from a foreign country. Could he come between me and my parents, after all? Accomplish what had eluded Mallman? In the weeks and months that followed, there would be no mutual seduction, no reliving that Freudian minuet. I'd come to a place like a gym, to change ancient habits that could lead me out of hiding these seven years. Under Dr. Cherian's guidance, I'd also started thyroid replacement. He was certain that my symptoms were a mirror image of the ones he'd read to me from his homeopathic dictionary under Thyroid Deficiency. Having simultaneously started with Carl and thyroid, we would never know just what was slowly bringing me up for air, changing the way I breathed and what I could imagine.

If I've identified my collapse at Abraham & Straus's necktie counter followed by my husband's acid, detached response as the trigger for my descent into agoraphobia, it's because framing the story gave me some control. And for some of us, being in control is more compelling than getting to the heart of what created our symptoms. If you can't control what's happening, you can control the narrative. Another young woman with hypoglycemia and thyroid disorder would not have gone under house arrest and her husband's disaffection would not have been answered with self-inflicted wounds. I'd been programmed for the public humiliation, for men not taking care, for not seeing strangers as kind. As Mallman so decisively proclaimed, phobias were my creation, to gain some power over the crazy mother and the dismissive husband—at high cost, but finally with Carl's help, an account I might settle.

I was years from discovering that phobias take up the space in which to feel rage and where that might lead us. They are the perfect distraction and do their job —to keep us from discovering whatever it is that scares us to death, to keep us frozen. They are where we park fears and fury. It's worth repeating.

25

My agent still behaved as if I would write again and invited us all Upstate for lunch. As jittery as I was, an outing was possible because the work with Carl had begun. To my amazement, I joined the conversation as if I'd never left my magazine life, giving no sign that I counted bricks or steps. His friend Peter, an attorney, sat opposite me, watching my every move and would call me at home the next day. And keep calling.

From the safety of my kitchen, encircled by toys and plants and crockery, my little boy in first grade, I bantered with my admirer but didn't dare confess I was house-bound. He'd met me on a Sunday afternoon with old friends, everyone at the table unaware I had this little problem of agoraphobia.

"I'm coming to Brooklyn to see another lawyer on Court Street. Can we meet for lunch?" His voice was pitch-perfect, business-like and urgent. I hesitated for a moment and then agreed to meet him on Atlantic Avenue at a Middle Eastern restaurant. A car service would get me there, and cabs heading north on Clinton Street would get me back. Not exactly one of my ordinary errands planned like fire drills, this was an outing anyone might think dangerous.

As I drew back the curtained entry to the shadowed dining room, it took a moment to see Peter seated at a corner table. He stood as I approached and smiled a serious smile from a serious fellow.

Scanning the menu, he took my hand absentmindedly, as if we were an old couple. The litigator laid out the facts: "I've been burned by my wife. She's with my best friend now. We're in proceedings."

Until now, all I knew was that they were separated, and he had his young sons on weekends. I hadn't pressed for more details in our phone calls because the very specter of separation made me queasy— happening all around me but still a hot potato that secretly meant women going nuts, being tied down and served divorce papers in mental hospitals, images that lodged themselves between me and temptation.

"You're not in the right place. When will you make a move?" If only Peter could have known the burlesque irony of his question. Moving was a daily meditation. How many steps to Frank's on the corner? How hard to meet him today? I told him I didn't know. And that I was sorry for misleading him.

"It's I who should be sorry. This is way too soon. I'm just allergic to adultery." And then, knowing Eckart spent many Sunday afternoons at his office, he asked,

"Can I bring my boys next weekend to meet Nico?"

The three boys played in the backyard, cautiously, and then with real excitement. We heard their calls, tossing the ball as we sat at the table with more ease than I'd expected. Peter's parents were White Russian émigrés. Fancy folk. His Eastern almond shaped eyes were merry as we interrupted one another. I was both relieved and anxious to, once again, feel the high of attraction, as I brushed past him to pour the tea and slice the cake.

The children's voices faded in and out as we flirted beneath the family photographs hung on the rosy brick: Eckart, bearded, his arm clasped tenderly around two-year-old Nico, both of them grinning, the three of us that same weekend in Washington, photographed in Gail's garden, Nico between us. Not more recent ones of the three of us, just Nico grinning, radiant, safe.

The excitement I felt was a relic from the past, before I'd become a mother. Once my son had arrived, lying down with anyone but Eckart wasn't even a fantasy, no matter how lonely I felt. In recent years, I'd never even imagined a moment like this, seated beside a man who was tempting me, with my little boy playing beneath the window. Open marriage was the rage in these mid-Seventies, and we knew a couple or two living it, but we also knew a few casualties of the experiment. The specter of breaking apart our little unit literally made me dizzy.

As he guided his sons towards the door, Peter leaned forward and lightly kissed my cheeks, as if we were Russian cousins. Nico raced to the long window to wave wildly, calling to both boys as they turned back, sticking out their tongues.

Later that week, Peter came for lunch on a school day. Like the litigator he was, he made a case for me to consider. Although we'd never even embraced, he wanted to be with me—someone he'd created, from the line drawing of our meeting Upstate, our phone visits, one lunch.

We circled the subject of attraction and my whereabouts: will you leave, will you stay? The table beneath the family photos was a life raft, keeping us safe. When finally we moved to the sofa, Peter drew me against his chest in a bear hug, the way he might have comforted one of his sons. He made no move to kiss me and held me too tightly to be exciting—an emergency, rather than the purposeful touch that seduces.

When he released me, he held my face in both hands and said, "I'm allergic, you know... I can't do this."

And I couldn't tell the truth, which was that I couldn't break from Eckart, who was keeping me dangerously safe without more reassurance from Peter, who was only urging a daring move, not a safe landing. And besides... the tiny little fact of my agoraphobia would send him flying, should he be included in my secret, which still kept me from dreaming of another life, let alone living it and which, unbeknownst to me, was keeping Eckart from his real self, his real life.

Did I miss my chance with Peter out of loyalty to Eckart, to Nico, or to my mother? Yes, my mother. Could I have left her behind, shrieking or eerily quiet, if I dared to have more than she'd ever had? Having kept my distance these last years, repelled and unable to forgive her, was I atoning by having less?

Was she standing beside me, on the stoop, as I watched Peter go down the steps, and when he turned to wave as Leonard had on the wharf? And when I closed the heavy front door?

26

The year in which I didn't leave for Peter had passed. Now in late April, leaves were in bud on Second Place, as they always were for my birthday. The night before, we'd decided where to celebrate that evening. I could manage to go to Nino's on Union Street without too much anxiety thanks to Carl, but still couldn't get off the block without hearing my heart, without the racing that came without warning. Eckart admitted he'd hoped for more progress by now and was alternately stoic or withdrawn. But this morning he smiled, as he got out of bed, and said, "I'll bring you tea."

It was Sunday and Nico was still sleeping, as he did on weekends, as if he knew he didn't have school. I turned towards the shutters and studied the filtered light, luxuriating in my Tangiers fantasy. Do all agoraphobics have images of a time before they were stricken, times of wandering, of adventure? Imaging the exotic when the ordinary is impossible?

I'll dress up tonight ... we'll have the sitter ... we'll take our time. The offer of tea in bed had brought back better times when Eckart had made the German fuss over birthdays ... always a candle, flowers, the gift set on the table ... learned in Potsdam and continued even during the war.

The first yowl came flying up from the kitchen at a pitch that could only mean one thing. Another cat had found its way in. I sprang out of bed and closed Nico's door, hoping our Tusie was on his bed. I stood on the landing and called out "Eckart" to break in, to remind him of me, of his sleeping son, as the screeching came louder than the year before. In a cold sweat, I waited for Nico's door to open, but when, mercifully, it remained closed, I sank to the floor.

This time it wasn't an ax. He'd stomped it to death... barefoot, flattening its body, breaking its jaw... seeing the blood run across the floor beneath the island with the Mexican tiles... with Tusie safe upstairs? Just for the hell of it? Had his wiring snapped? The first time, I'd told myself, he'd lost control even though Tusie had escaped and was out of danger. This time I was the cat beneath his feet.

"Are you crazy, too? Is this how you'll get me to leave?" Was what I should have asked him if I'd been ready for his reply. I've often wondered if he was so entrapped in his inauthentic life that his only way out would be if he got *me* to leave? Could that have been driving his rage, even today, just a year from the last killing?

Again the cat was wrapped in newspapers and put in the garbage can I would pass whenever I closed the garden gate at the sidewalk. This time there is no dialogue to report, no aftermath with Eckart because a kind of amnesia has replaced the actual film, and I don't want to invent here.

I can tell you that I didn't tell anyone because I knew what the advice would be. And so being a good secret-keeper, I put this one away. Not because I was so selfless and wanted Nico to live with his father under any circumstances but because I was unable to imagine each day on my own with my little boy. That specter was more horrifying than the one of the cat's jaws flattened, its blood running across the parquet.

I will, in a kind of penance for my paralysis, hold the image forever and at times, when stroking another kitty, feeling its soft bones, get a flash of those howls, retriggering the moment, to relive its pain. The least I can do.

At my next session, Carl and I were at loggerheads. I'd decided I needed revelation, a place to bring news that wasn't just about being outside the house, exposed. He, the good cognitive behavior therapist, would not oblige. I'd grown to distrust his soulful, mournful face. His eyes which, unlike Mallman's, were steel gray like Eckart's.

"He's killed another cat. Like the time just before we went to see my Dad in San Miguel." I paused, not for effect, but because I already regretted bringing this to him. I'd learned in this year what Carl would deal with and what was off limits. Anything having to do with my marriage was of no interest to him.

"Well, you know you have a choice: you can collapse, regress, give back the strides you've been making or move on." He clasped his hands in the usual way, like a rabbi.

"I need to tell you how he did it." I leaned forward.

"What will that do for you, to rehearse it, to relive it so it can have even more power over you? We've been in the business of giving you back the power you gave up." He lowered his voice, instead of raising it for emphasis. Did he want to let me in on a secret?

"Giving me the details won't change anything and will only freeze those moments for you... *We need to let you let them go!*" The volume returned as he shifted in his chair.

"Carl, this feels like your old story about me getting better so Eckart will be more comfortable... we need to look at this and how it makes me feel... otherwise this is just about a formula... and if I stick to your formula I'll be able to move around but if I can move around... " My throat tightened, tears filled my eyes.

"Yes, Linda, you'll have choices." Carl nodded, taking the deep breath I couldn't. In that moment I wanted to hurl Mallman at him, shame him into more gentle collaboration, the talking cure.

He nodded again, bowed his head and sighed, "If you refuse to move through your fear, we're wasting energy here. If after nearly a year you're still not convinced this can work, that you can resume a normal life... we should look at that and make some decisions." Now he mustered a smile, the apologetic executioner.

I gripped the arms of the chair as the room began to blur. I might as well have been in the middle of Atlantic Avenue. He'd never wanted a description of a panic attack, now he was a witness. My face glistened. My heart raced. Carl didn't make a move towards me. There was no Kleenex offering.

"Breathe. Focus on the window. Breathe." His voice was steady, as steady as I needed it to be.

"You've always said it lasts forty-five minutes... that the adrenaline will run out." I was talking to the carpet which seemed like a safe place at the moment.

"And it will, although we only have forty more minutes today." He smiled again. "You have the choice . . . take this cat killing as a challenge. Accept that reliving it today won't take you where you need to be. You need to do something you're really afraid of now. You have the tools, you won't die. You might have to admit to how much of a survivor you are." He allowed himself a grin, "Little Linda."

"And then what?" My breath was even. My hands weren't clammy.

"Well, you're not ready to pilot a helicopter over the harbor . . . How about walking up Clinton, all the way to Atlantic." He might as well have been a travel agent, suggesting a trip through Tibet.

"Okay, I'll put that on the to-do list." I smiled my father's Brooklyn Bridge-smile and walked unsteadily to the door. The Akita was heaving against the basement gate. How had this behaviorist trained his dog to know when the sessions were over?

27

As the airport taxi approached Munich, eight-year-old Nico announced it looked just like New Jersey, until with a dramatic sweep of his arm, he declared the stucco houses crisscrossed with wood to be "German!"

From her kitchen window, I watched my sister-in-law, Andrea, gathering forget-me-nots in the garden, which gave her so much pleasure. The one place where her anxieties were at bay, where she wasn't ruled by them, where her terrible war years were left behind. She hurried back to arrange the pale blue flowers in a pewter jug, set on the painted chest serving as a coffee table: the constant source of irritation for our mother-in-law, Karin, who believed the choice of the trunk was the ultimate symbol of Andrea's refusal to create a presentable home, but instead lived with my brother-in-law and their nine-year-old daughter like *studenten*!

If not for that blue trunk, we would be celebrating Karin's seventy-fifth birthday at their house, instead of in the faded splendor of the sprawling Hotel Kaiserin Elisabeth, overlooking Lake Amsee, near Munich.

Amidst fraying, gray velvet, my husband stood to toast his mother in English (for me and his son), to tell twenty-five guests that her life had been a triumph, after all. Nico heard his father's voice break, as Eckart recounted the loss of his own father. By now, our son knew the story of his grandfather's death. At three, Nico had watched Eckart's eyes fill with tears as Memorial Day images filled our T.V. screen. He'd listened solemnly to Eckart's description of a battle in the Polish woods, his father's tank ambushed, and Heinz shot in that tank. Without a word, Nico had reached beneath the sofa for his Tonka truck and zoomed away from the screen with its rows of crosses, from his father's crumpled face.

Now, with his glass held high, Eckart continued, "After years of uncertain fortune... many losses and resumptions... *Mutti*, you begin your seventy-fifth year in good health, financial security, and surrounded by well-wishers." He bowed stiffly, smiled, but didn't move towards her, seated at his elbow.

I'd never seen him hug her, although he had on many occasions praised her for saving them from the British, the Russians, and the Americans when he and his brother were so small. Her most sterling trait had been her ability to guess where the troops would land: to keep them safe, but then to be a most unsafe only parent, ever correcting, ever teaching, and ever punishing.

I was seated next to Ebo, one of Eckart's cousins, whose forehead was marked with what looked like a crater wound, received in the car accident which blinded him when he was seventeen. The sunken spot on his forehead throbbed with a life of its own and his eyes stared so intelligently it was hard to believe he was in the dark. He turned toward my voice. His father, a retired Siemens executive, was on my left. I wondered, as I always did, when faced with an older German, if he had had Nazi sympathies and then thought... if he had, he's paid. Ebo's mother was killed in the accident that blinded him. She also left behind his baby brother, who was to grow but not enough. This noble family was to bear the trial of raising a thalidomide dwarf as well as a blind child. Like Ebo, Gerhardt the second son seemed to accept his fate, looking directly up into my eyes as he offered the stump of his hand.

Karin had briefed us on the family history and wanted us to appreciate the sacrifice of the dowager grandmother, now dead, who marshaled the motherless family, and was always formally dressed by eight o'clock in the morning. Karin had raised her voice for emphasis, "She was *immer* corseted and wearing her jewels, opening the door for the cleaning lady!" sniffed Karin, "She was a person of correct education."

I glanced down at my Indian print cotton dress, which I knew was not Karin's idea of the right costume for the occasion, but because of the work in the shadowy Park Slope office, I smiled without apology.

That evening, after Nico had fallen asleep, we lay on the sateen bedspread recapping the party. Eckart marveled at his family's survival as he stared out at the dark lawn—the "fat green" as he liked to call grass. As abruptly as he could be cutting and remote, he could suddenly include me, as he did that night. I could still be moved by him, by the family we'd made, ever a pushover for reunion. Besides, it had been in bisected West Berlin that I'd shopped and cooked, lived full-time with a man for the first time, and flirted with the idea of never going home. But that week I couldn't be amongst them without feeling torn. Was I a universal cosmopolite, or a Jew who could never trust even the "good Germans"? With his thinly veiled anti-semitism, Eckart didn't qualify as one of the "good" Germans. I knew they existed. I'd met the ardent students, had coffee with them, and talked long into the night around the kitchen table on Niebuhrstrasse. But they weren't the one I lived with. Even in the midst of this celebration and feeling sympathy for many of them, I was sure I'd have been one of the ones who didn't act, didn't leave in time.

For most of the days, Eckart mostly ignored me or was repeatedly snappish, directing our schedule, the all-too-packed itinerary. When the Germans celebrate they do it like everything else, with purpose.

After another of his outbursts, I decided to nap instead of walking with the others round the lake one more time. As I fell fitfully into a mid-afternoon sleep, I dreamt...

I am nine years old, once again in the ranch house in California's San Fernando Valley, where my father has taken us to avoid being in New York while his older brother dies of stomach cancer. This house feels like a play house. I cross the linoleum in bare feet, noticing how smoothly I can glide. Then I cross the sun-scorched patio to feel the cool grass under my feet. I'm under the grape arbor where my father has set planks across saw horses to make a table and has arranged brightly painted (by him) nail kegs, to serve as seats. I am captivated by the sunlight, the soft air, and the fun of our meals under the grape arbor. Just before the dream ends, I tell myself we are the happiest of families. Everyone Under The Tent.

"Get yourself together. We will be late again. You know my mother gets upset when we are late." Eckart stood above me.

I saw his oxford shirt, his tweed slacks, and the gleam of his belt buckle. I wasn't yet back from the sunny dream and wanted to return to the table beneath the grape arbor. I reached for his hand and hoped our son didn't see him pull it back. I got up, smoothing Nico's hair as I passed him on my way to the bathroom to redraw my eye liner. My interest in eye makeup was a small sign of return I will only know later, when I'm using L'Air du Temps again, my favorite cologne, no longer acrid as it had been these years since Nico's birth.

As the taxi sped along the Belt Parkway, in Brooklyn, cluttered with junk and debris missing from German highways, Nico shouted, "We're home! Home!" His voice filled with familiarity, authority. We'd missed the blooming of our neighbor's pear tree, whose petals were strewn in our back yard, leaving trails of white everywhere. The first heat wave of the summer was once more telling New Yorkers that their hope for a real spring was canceled.

As we turned the key, the phone rang.

"Sooo good to hear your voice," my mother crooned, as I steeled myself for her grievance list, the calamities she's endured these days. Thanks to Carl, I now had some distance, which came not only from accomplishing tasks he and I cooked up but from his insistence that Bea could not perform them without medication because she was chemically unbalanced, and I was not.

He had accomplished what Mallman failed to do . . . beginning to separate me from a woman whose illness had filled me with longing for the other mother, the one before the violence . . . before she became a woman whose mean streak (for whatever reasons) had joined with her illness to declare me the wrong baby all these years later. Psychosis, I will learn, is not always accompanied with cruelty. Or as we know, not all drunks are mean drunks.

Now I had tools, forged from the dimly lit office, if I dared to use them.

28

In the fall I still wasn't fixed but tired of phobias being my self-description. I reminded myself each morning, after Nico left for school, "You've always thought there was a perfect time to write, and for every reason you've stopped." Until one day, I went to the safety of my bed with a thermos of tea and, not at my desk, began to work again.

A writing friend had asked me now that Nico was in first grade, why wasn't I writing? If returning to magazine work wasn't possible, why not work on fiction? Did I secretly believe my discoveries would be so searing that my fingers would burn as I tapped the keys? That the short stories I'd created in college, where young girls spied on their beloveds from thickets of blueberry bushes, weren't just efforts of a young observer, but were the evidence: of how I'd learned to leave the room, take cover, make a quick exit before full catastrophe, choose the safety of dire prediction over uncontrollable surprise, of how I'd become an escape artist, unable to say what I meant, to know what I felt, and even worse for a writer, too cautious to risk discovery.

No matter how many times I'd picked up (like a good-enough mother) the pieces of Bea's drama, I'd often felt childlike, unsure, my judgments and choices suspect. At times I secretly longed to be that seven-year old girl dancing around the coffee table to the songs of *"Oklahoma"* . . . as the wind came sweeping off the plain into our apartment half a block from Washington Square. One moment in charge of managing the unmanageable, the next longing to be cradled, held, as I'd held my son. A wild ride that could make the steadiest person dizzy, and we know by now, I wasn't firmly planted, but I was beginning to see that my mother's story wasn't mine ... sailing on *The Liberté,* wrapped in wildflowers, strapped down for midnight ambulance rides. The middle of the movie was her movie, after all.

Although panic and dread of panic could invade me, I was comforted by what Colette called "earthly delights" ... buoyed by following the sun's path across our brownstone and by imagining its fall, a few blocks west, into the Hudson behind the Red Hook piers. The image of the river opening into the harbor and beyond was tantalizing. I knew what it looked like and could conjure it up although I hadn't seen the sun set on Atlantic Avenue in years, not since I was pregnant and walked up Clinton with Eckart to a Middle Eastern restaurant to celebrate our move to Second Place.

One evening our psychotherapist friend, Beverly, came from the Slope for dinner. It was her husband's night to take their children to his new place. She arrived, freshly showered, gleaming the way we all used to, before going out for dinner meant first feeding kids and hurrying into a dress. In her newly separated status, she, the super Mom, the super Renovator, had softened, and to my surprise, extravagantly praised our stalled renovation.

But as I diced and chopped, Beverly got to the point. She'd known for years I was hiding a lot from my son. With Eckart upstairs with Nico, she seized her moment.

"This is not Victorian England, Victorian anything! Kids get everything anyway."

I looked up from my perfect slices, unprepared to defend a decision made at the onset of the phobias, when Nico had begun making whole sentences. Beverly came to the edge of the counter and stared me down.

"Hiding is always dangerous. It confuses everything. So, you have this problem. You are hiding it from your own child. Tell him. So, you're only human. Then he can be human, too." She sat her glass down and popped a zucchini spear into her mouth.

My knees went as weak as if I were on the street alone or in a supermarket. Before I could defend myself, Eckart joined us. As he poured more wine, she went on.

"My kids have lived with so much tension. It's better now," Beverly lifted her chin defiantly, as if we might dare cross-examine her. "I always had to cry in the bathroom with the water running so I wouldn't upset Richard!"

She went on to describe her new guy, how great it was to be able to say, "Okay, now I want the house to myself!" Sometimes, I love being in bed alone... how wonderful to lie there and not have someone touching you."

She was reclaiming the whole house, even its walls with new colors. The children, in her version, were old enough to fit into the new order of non-order. Her daughters, she observed, were so unlike us.

"What can I say about Samantha? She says her friend Janie, also has a vaginal discharge! Ten years old, right? And she's freer than we ever were. No problem with the nude beach on the Cape this summer.

Samantha saw hundreds of penises and in a few days wasn't interested anymore," she paused, holding her glass high, "unless there was a really big one or enormous balls."

Eckart and I never once looked at each other as she went on to attack her old married life as zealously as she'd once papered the walls of their Park Slope brownstone. Before dessert, Beverly declared herself free of conflict, living her goals of feeling, crying, really living. Despite her insistence on her transformation, I saw the same woman I'd known in her ninth month, six feet up on a ladder and a few weeks later, breast feeding her baby, as she ladled steaming soup for her guests.

Predictably, the specter of the single life, made me as queasy as Peter's attraction. I couldn't congratulate the phobias for a job well-done because it would be more years before I'd get it—see how disorders and addictions can hold tight what needs to be untangled, broken.

Nico was asking for a puppy. I took him up on his wish and started researching miniature dachshunds. He knew about my Cokey and Penny and wanted to be sure this one would be his. He was eight and wanted his big boy dog even if it would weigh less than ten pounds fully grown.

When we arrived at the home breeder's, at the end of Long Island, Mrs. Beale had tied a wide, red ribbon on the female, just to make sure we didn't attach to anyone else scampering around her kitchen. The gleaming patent leather pup, with the hound face I'd asked for, was hidden behind the lipstick red ribbon. Even without her tag, we'd have chosen Josie.

As soon as we were home, Eckart picked a red towel to wrap her snugly and tucked Josie into the corner of our sofa, explaining to Nico that if swaddling made babies feel safe, it was the right thing for his new puppy. Before he left them alone together, he told his son, "She will be calm this way. She will feel safe so far from her mother." In that moment I didn't see the cats' killer. But later, with the lights out and Josie curled in my armpit, I heard their cries.

Josie had arrived in January and for two months piddled on paper. In March it was time to train her, as best as any dachshund is ever trained, and to get her used to other dogs, to the pavement.

The first time I walked her alone, to the end of the block, I kept my eyes on her red sweater, her tail held high. The light-headed queasiness was there, the old sensation like a lingering scent, but I followed Josie and let her take me as far as the corner, feeling the power, Cokey and 10th Street, my four-year-old self in charge.

My childhood doxies came in flashes, curled in my lap, snoozing in the sunlight, Josie's antics were familiar. Doxies know where and when to emerge from blankets, one ear caught in the folds. In those first weeks of her life in our family, I became her mother, Eckart her father, and Nico her sibling. Just as my infant had reminded me of my puppies, Josie now reminded me of falling in love with my baby. Like the young and elderly in hospitals, visited and cheered by dogs, I was marvelously distracted.

Predictably, my mother was intensely jealous of the pup. "Now a dog keeps you busy! I can't find my keys... no food... the doorman, the doorman, that sonofabitch won't answer the phone!"

She was back to harassing the staff at her building. There would be more letters of complaint, even threats of eviction for disturbance. Carl had desensitized me to flooding panic, but he hadn't dulled her impact. The full throttle of her still made me as edgy as a barnyard animal before a storm.

"Every time I call, you're busy! Busy! With that dog! Always too busy... let me tell you something..." she croaked.

I could hear her breathing and see her eyes roaming her studio apartment, the shambles that surrounded her. Was she bothered by the disheveled array crowding every surface? Did she yearn for the simplicity she could create only in her Avery-like paintings, where flat surfaces met each other in unexpected, inspired color? Like the one with a woman seated at a table on which there is one large strawberry, titled *The Picnic*, a hauntingly lonely painting. If she'd ever been able to *say* she was lonely, afraid, to describe instead of sending words like bullets, I'd have come nearer instead of fiercely keeping my distance, in the doorway, if she had just not been so menacing and dangerous.

Josie was more or less house-trained, and now the short walks to the corner were routine. At the start of spring, the red sweater was put away and her shiny coat was admired by our neighbors. For the first time in years, I could smile back, say a few words, and walk on without a quaver, a pulsing in my throat. A tiny thyroid pill and many hours with Carl were bringing me back from a web of circumstances that would never be fully identified, like parts of speech.

Carl's job was to get me back outside, doing regular errands, which had turned streets into rivers, supermarkets into breath-taking challenges. The ordinary had become extraordinary, long before *panic attacks* were in the language.

Although the marriage troubles should have been brought to therapy, Carl continually discouraged that. He was uncomfortable with any reference to being untouched and still insisted that if I got fixed there was a chance for the marriage, as if I'd driven my husband away. As if Eckart's aloofness and absence were simply a matter of retaliation and could be reversed if I behaved better.

Unwittingly, Carl's assumptions were to fuel my belief that if I'd been a more attractive package, Eckart wouldn't have made his middle-aged confession, even if the information was old news to him. Carl's limitations would keep clear of the tangle of my mother and me and my mysterious husband, of the price I was paying for protection. Crossing a wide avenue was the only goal he could promote.

29

"Let's write Lupe loves Ramon on the Great Wall of China!" Nico cried to Josh as they raced around our small back garden. Despite my fears of ruining his childhood, Nico was having one after all. Not the picket fence one I'd pretended to have but something just the same. He was a third-grader, full of beans, but must have sensed his mom wasn't okay, was in some way hiding.

"Mom, I wanna take Josie round the block." He looked me straight in the eye. I'd been dreading this moment for weeks, sensing the time was coming when he'd need to get off our block, turn the corner, and move around the neighborhood. Josie was just four months old and still a target for one of the larger dogs who strained at their leashes but were walked by ten-year-olds.

"We'll go together." I said as if it was the most regular idea, that we go out in public, just the two of us taking a helicopter out over the harbor.

Would the puppy protect me from the crazy feeling I was sure would overtake me, from sweat rolling down the middle of my back, from being unable to swallow, unable to speak, even another blackout, the specter I'd been keeping all these years from my little boy?

"I've got the leash!" He called triumphantly from the hallway. Josie scampered across the slippery floor into his arms. For an instant, he bent his face to hers, letting her lick his cheeks. Then he snapped the leash to her collar.

Nearly six o'clock, folks were coming home from work, their arms filled with newspapers and paper bags from Court Street shopping. Tired and glad to be back on their block, back in Carroll Gardens from Manhattan, the other universe. Pots were boiling, children were being screamed back into their houses, and soon, after supper, the stoops would be crowded until the light faded later and later as spring unfolded.

"Ma, she's hard to hold! She's all over the place." Nico put on his brakes, digging in his heels, holding her leash tight. He was grinning at his dog and feeling *his* power.

We turned up Clinton and had to go one more block to Third Place, where we turned left and continued towards Henry Street. Once we got to Henry, we were only a block from the corner of Second Place. When we passed Frank's we were almost home. The danger was not in the street: the mountain lion still lived in me. Instead of admiring roof lines and the lingering streaks of rose in the sky, I kept my eyes on Josie and Nico's baseball cap. The points I'd chosen for this voyage, baby steps.

"She loved that walk. Pretty soon, I'll go myself." Nico announced as he snapped off her leash and ran down the stoop to have a few more catches with Josh in the dusk.

Like money troubles, illness always separates, isolates. The improvement of either catastrophe is of real interest only to the one who's lived it. For years I'd gone places with Eckart, steadying myself with my arm on his, comfortably uncomfortable. But I'd never dared risk Nico seeing me in another attack in public, the Abraham & Straus event repeated, this time his mother splayed out on the cement. Not in control. Not reliable. This round-the-block walk had been a test run. I needed to go farther with him and without Josie as a beacon, far enough from Second Place to call it *going out with Nico*, to bring it to Carl like the trophy it would be.

A few weeks after he'd become Josie's round-the-block-walker, I asked Nico if he'd like to go up to the Heights with me. It was a balmy Saturday morning, and his mysterious father had gone to the office.

"We never walk to Montague. What are we going to do when we get there?" He looked at me quizzically, genuinely puzzled.

His acceptance of our boundaries made me cringe. The abnormal had become the norm for my most beloved person.

"It's a nice day for a walk. We'll check out the Variety Mart. Don't you need a new bat for Little League?" I sounded like a commercial.

As we headed for the vestibule, the phone rang. Nico had heard enough of my replies to my mother's long attacks to know the ringing meant ambush, could keep me there, could leave me pale, teary. I held up my index finger to say silently *just a minute,* as if the room was bugged and the wires would take my words across the river to 72nd Street. He scowled, exasperated for all those other times and for now, when we have a plan. He, too, was captured by the magical possibility of being overheard in his own living room and whispered, "Tell her you can't talk. You're busy."

I let the answering machine pick up, hurling my mother into the room.

"You must be there! You're never far from that house, from that family of yours! I'm sitting up here … there's a man across the street … in that same window, pointing a gun!"

She paused, gasped, "How can you? You're my lifeline, my darling daughter!" and then snarled, "You son of a bitch!"

Nico pulled his cap down over his face, as if it could keep him safe. He slumped onto the sofa expecting me to be busy for an hour. I surprised both of us as I popped the cap back on his shiny hair, and propelled him towards the door, checking that Josie was snug on her pillow.

Passing the hall mirror I saw the young woman who'd lowered the shades, closed the heavy door, now four years older. She'll never divorce her mother as her father had advised, but today she was going out with her boy. The wrong baby walked past the rasping voice, not to teach a lesson but because finally the craziness had clicked. If this is illness talking, it isn't about me and Bea. It isn't personal. I can tell you this in the third person because part of the "click" is that I could walk on by without abandoning her. As Eckart often said about my phobias, "Take the night off; they'll be there in the morning." I'll take her calls and continue managing the unmanageable to keep her out of mental hospitals but not today. Today I was taking the day off.

I opened the door without a hint of free-falling to the cement. The sun was strong on my cheek as I looked left across the stoops to Court Street, moving right along to catch up to my son. Heading up Clinton Street, Bea's voice was still with me and I assumed with Nico. I put my hand on his shoulder.

"Grandma has problems. She gets things mixed up. You know she loves you." I said firmly, as we walked north to Atlantic Avenue.

"Yeah, I know," he said without conviction, shrugging my hand away and leaping to touch a branch a few feet above.

Trotting along, kicking at stray stones, he changed the subject, telling me about his art class. He wasn't complaining as I once did about the awful Pearl of my Little Red days. He was boasting: "My teacher says I can draw anything. She says I'm an artist!" He looked up from beneath his baseball cap. Before I could reply, he made it clear, "But I'm going to be an athlete, not some sissy artist."

We reached Amity Street in Cobble Hill: a quarter of a mile, a Saturday afternoon in May, a regular day with regular folks setting out on their errands. Under the leafy canopies, people chatting, glad to see each other, glad to be out without coats, not in any drama, just blessedly ordinary, how you feel after an operation, after needles and tubes, when washing dishes and vacuuming suddenly becomes a privilege. Until you break your vow and begin to complain again.

I'd nearly relaxed into the walk when the cues of panic began: my throat started to close. My chest tightened. The ringing in my ears invaded and my vision blurred. If I'd been on a racing train, I'd have pulled the brake. I stood still in the middle of the sidewalk, determined not to lean against the nearest building. *This will pass... time-limited... breathe... just breathe.* Terrified of the darkness about to take me down, I filled my lungs and focused on my son's blue jacket.

Nico had sprinted to the corner and was pointing to the light to get me to hurry to get me to cross Atlantic Avenue with him, to get to the Variety Mart, to get the bat! A regular errand ... *Let it go ... let this craziness fly into the air ... breathe ... and walk ... wave to your son ... let him know you're with him.*

My vision cleared, but not the ringing. When I joined him at the curb, my face was streaked with sweat.

"What a slowpoke you are, Mom!" He jabbed my hip for emphasis and firmly pressed the "Cross" button.

Unsteady, lightheaded, I looked left down Atlantic Avenue to the harbor, to the skyline beyond. An American flag swirled in the breeze. The light changed, we followed the few people ahead of us. A younger mother pushed a carriage carrying a serene baby girl. Although there was a carriage between them, the connection between the baby and her mother was obvious. They were in the high gear of new love.

At the Variety Mart, Nico picked out his bat with the assurance of a long-time player. Little League will enthrall him for at least another year.

"Mom, let's get the bus back. I'm sick of walking. I want to show it to Josh."

A packed bus down Court Street was more than I'd bargained for, but the high of *not fainting* carried me the long blocks to the bus stop. Nico took some practice swings with the new bat, creating a wide swath around us. However shakily, I was moving along with my boy, who didn't seem to be paying attention to the big event.

"Hey, I know you! You're from Second Place, right?" A retired longshoreman who hung out at Frank's, was at the curb. "I'm never far from the block, but today ... so nice ... so nice, the weather ..." He smiled at both of us, not recognizing the same woman he'd helped onto the bus heading for Abraham & Straus that June morning years ago. I didn't remind him. I smiled back, shifting my weight from one foot to the other, filled with dread. As the bus pulled up, I saw it was crammed, standing room only.

"Let's wait for the next one." I patted Nico's shoulder to hold him back.

"Come on, Mom! Josh's waiting for me!" He was grinning, but his eyes were piercing as only our children's eyes can be.

I felt the press of jackets, hips, and packages, smelled tobacco on leather jackets. The next bus could be empty, but as I looked into my son's dark eyes, I followed him onto the bus. The coins dropped into the box, my heart raced, and my throat started to close. *Breathe out slowly* I could hear Carl whisper.

Breathing deeply, I met the gaze of the other passengers, who saw not a panic-stricken phobic, just a regular Mom taking her son home. As we crossed Atlantic Avenue, I dared to look all the way down to the harbor again, this time imagining the open sea. The sun was setting behind Manhattan's skyline. Nico saw it, too, and worried that his game would be cut short. I touched his cheek lightly and said, "There's plenty of time. Supper can wait." And kept to myself the good racing of my heart.

30

Six months later we had moved back to the Heights, to a penthouse created out of the attic on the rooftop of a 1906 building. Small French windows faced the Statue of Liberty and the harbor. The World Trade Center was the intrusion on the historic view. Although I was still shaky and could only navigate the few blocks leading to the Promenade and the Manhattan skyline, I was also exhilarated enough to create (with the help of a local contractor) a glass dining room on the terrace. An architect friend pronounced the place "the most romantic apartment in New York."

It was in this apartment on an early March morning, while Nico still slept, that Eckart confessed he was in love with a man. Once again, my vagus nerve sent me into instant darkness. Unable to see, in a cold sweat, I lay beside him trembling. I couldn't know, in those few moments, that we would continue to live as a family for three years while he lived a gay life. What I did know in those moments was that my getting better was what had given him a shot at living his true life, and he'd taken it.

"I met this black guy in Washington Square, near the arch." He was talking to the ceiling with his hands propped behind his head on the pillow.

Washington Square! My Washington Square! I could see the arch and the fountain a few yards away where I'd played every afternoon after school, after walking up MacDougal Street with my Mom. I was focused on that image instead of on the news which will change my life as surely as the birth of my son had.

Nico's room was next to the entrance of the apartment, and it would be there he would awaken to hear his father coming back at three in the morning, after having had a quick supper with us, before heading out to the gay bars in the Village. My Village. Why, you might ask, did you agree to this? The answer is multiple as in multiple choice on the SATs. Just as I couldn't imagine managing without him when Nico was just toddling, I couldn't imagine living without him even knowing he'd be coming home, even in the middle of the night. Although we hadn't slept entwined since my pregnancy, his body next to mine fed the illusion that we might again. Besides, twenty years with a closeted man had taken its toll. The days of my wild escapades were long gone, the impetuous young woman who had lain down with men she barely knew had evaporated, as if she'd never existed and in her place was a daily test of how "normal" she could be, out of the brownstone and back in the Heights. The third person is not a typo but rather the way I felt: shattered, split—like an abstract painting. When I attempted to go back to writing for magazines, I was shocked to learn that payment would be the same it had been ten years before when I'd quit to be a full-time Mom, The Madonna. But the economics weren't nearly as powerful as the images of my mother storming across the terrace with no Eckart to stop her. I was far from seeing that the roots of my need for protection went deeper than recent history with my unhinged mother. Although not raging when I was an infant and toddler, she was absent, distracted by the chemistry that would erupt a few years later. I hadn't been safe in her arms.

I agreed to anything he asked for, hoping this was a phase, a mid-life crisis that would recede as stealthily as it had come. This is why I was in the East Village on a Sunday afternoon entering a gallery exhibition of nude black men. Eckart hadn't prepared me. He'd said we were going to a friend's photo show. I assumed it was a new gay friend but never assumed close up shots of penises flaccid or erect. After putting a paper cup of wine in my hand, he wandered off to greet young men he knows or will know. I was not the only woman in the room, but the others were younger, laughing and at ease.

"Why didn't you warn me?" I asked as he started the car.

"Oh, I didn't know it was a nude show. Don't make a big deal of this."

The next weekend we were off to the Jamaican section of Brooklyn. Eckart said he was looking for the shop where he can buy special vitamins. I am so naïve that it only occurs to me as I write this that he meant drugs. He navigated the crowded streets until he found the shop. I was told to sit where I am. As I waited for him to return I was struck by how invisible I'd become. That he would take me along on this errand without a worry that I might question him, object, or even draw the line at what he was into. When his latest boyfriend uses the intercom in our lobby to ask if he is home, I know I've been erased. Now his teenage boys have access to our home, if only from the lobby. Our name is next to Penthouse North, and I expect more than a phone call.

The nightly exits and entrances became routine. I was so determined to keep this news from my ten, eleven, and then twelve-year-old son that I didn't do what might have brought everything into the open. I don't ask if he hears his father coming home in the middle of the night and if it worries him and signals that we are no longer a family.

The summer he is nineteen and about to enter his third year at Princeton, Eckart tells Nick he is gay, and his son tells me later that day that he blacked out or had a vagus reaction.

Decades later, Nick will tell me I got it wrong. He didn't blackout. He told his father that he loved him. And assumed his handsome, macho father had left for another woman.

These same decades later I will regret all that was hidden which sent Nico into hiding his anger for both of us as well as being unprepared for the treacherous path he'll be on in college when AIDS has exploded and no one knows much of anything, when superstition and misinformation reigns. When your gay father is an explosive burden, as you start to date the prize girls who've made it into the once all-male Ivy League, you may generalize and decide that those prize specimens are not for you.

In addition to my fear of falling, which was a visceral metaphor for being on my own with my son, Eckart's compulsion to revisit his decision fed my hope that this was all mid-life crisis and we would weather it, save the family and finally be a couple. At odd moments, early in the morning or having a drink, before dinner, on the terrace he would return to Germany.

265

"When I was growing up and we were living in those castles of my mother's friends from boarding school, all those "vons," it wasn't a big deal for husbands to be "bi" and to have their boyfriends. The wives went on with the family life and affairs were just part of that… even during the war." He mostly talked to the ceiling or the horizon as he had when he confessed he was in love with a man but it was clear he wanted me to know that what he was doing would not have been a big deal in his mother country. Here in Brooklyn Heights it was a big deal although hardly any of our friends knew what had changed. This was not Bloomsbury and I was not an accomplished writer. We were an ordinary troubled couple who just happened to have moved to the most romantic apartment in the city. If real estate defines you (not a reliable anthropological tool), the penthouse with the glass dining room told our friends we'd survived the brownstone stop and start renovation and had landed on our feet—ten floors above Henry Street, with a view of the harbor and Manhattan. And yes… the Statue of Liberty.

Although AIDS was in full flourish, we continued to have occasional protected sex. Not love making, sex. Our bed was crowded with images of men giving him what I assumed he really wanted. There was no way I could compete as I might have if he was having an affair with a woman but never having felt treasured or valuable to him would have made that impossible. When we lived in West Berlin and then married in New York, I'd made a bargain with myself. What drove the bargain home was his protection from my mother, and despite my father's warning, finding a man who wasn't in any way disturbed with knowing who she was. Unbeknownst to me, the deeper need to get what she could never give had been transferred to the *unavailable*, tall, blond German. This information could have changed the story, but there was no one in my life to suggest, gently, that I was marrying my mother. When Günter Grass asked, "What are you doing with this *student*?" he had the instinct to ask what I was avoiding. The brilliant, narcissistic artist took a moment to attempt to release me from the troubled course I was on. In 1977 when he was in New York to promote The Flounder... he sent me a note inviting me to a reading. I was not moving off Second Place alone and never responded.

Weeks before Eckart made his confession, we'd been embracing and he'd held my face in his hands to tell me that, finally, our bodies belonged together. I heard the words and remained entwined but silent as it didn't sound like him. Decades later, when his brother came from Munich for Eckart's memorial service, Joachim will tell me Eckart had been a liar from childhood... *finally our bodies belonged together* came rushing back. This at breakfast, a few hours before the memorial, as I passed the biscuits to my brother-in-law.

This same brother-in-law had been put in charge of his younger brother during the war when, despite the daily bombing raids, the fatherless boys were allowed to roam the countryside around their village in northern Germany. They stepped across dead cows and horses, peeked into basements where the civilian dead were awaiting burial. When the war ended, they were sent to boarding school, as their mother had been; where Joachim continued to watch over Eckart who couldn't sleep, and spent the nights listening to the chiming of the church bells. Joachim, the guardian, who will finally call his brother out: the liar.

After nearly three years of living the lie, Eckart bought a studio coop nearby and left the sale contract on his dresser where Nico will find it and discover his father is leaving us. This, too, I will only know years later. The afternoon Eckart packed his things, throwing shoes and books together into cardboard boxes, Nico was on the squash court smashing balls against the walls. By then he had become a teen competitor and the three walled court was where he let fly the anger he'd been holding for years. Anger at his AWOL Dad and anger at his needy Mom who leaned on him more than she could know. When, mercifully, the years swallow up many details of that time, the sight of Eckart throwing shoes and books into cartons will remain—on the run, finally off to his real life.

VI

31

In the early 1990s, in my early 50s, I arrived in the Hudson Valley as a refugee from Brooklyn Heights, unable to drive and never having lived in a house alone. The doorman was nowhere in sight. I had moved to an 1850 cottage in the village of Rhinebeck with my four animals but no husband or child or career. I had left the home ground of Brooklyn and Manhattan and come to a place where I had one beloved college friend—a risky business.

It was to be a year of multiple losses: my uterus; Nick (no longer Nico), had graduated and moved to L.A.; the death of our nineteen-year-old cat; and finally, most importantly, the death of my mother, whose manic depression had eluded treatment and left both of us too worn down for her old age. My mother had come to refer to me as her mother, an irony lost on her caregivers holding down the fort on East 72nd Street. When she died, a few months after my move, I was left in a void, no longer worrying about where she was or what she was up to. When the woman I'd allowed to be the interrupter was gone, I could see her even more as a victim and not the abuser she had been. Instead of seeing her as mean, it was life that could be mean, giving some the equipment for loving, denying it to others.

At times I was light-headed and dizzy, having balance problems and hints of the old agoraphobia. But because my nature wants to come to the party, I could admit to my old addiction to drama and chaos and let go of my gloom. Forego it completely? Not a chance. But having discovered that phobia is where we park our fears and fury, the prospect of coming into the room, not running for cover, occurred more and more. And not so mysteriously, my relationship with my mother kept getting better. Her paintings were on my walls. I'd made sure she had one show, at seventy, to give her those moments when others would see her as a painter, an artist, not an unhinged crazy. A few days before the opening she said, "I don't know what to wear. I don't know how to look like an artist." I found a turquoise silk shift (lithium had blown her up) and a pale turquoise beaded necklace. That evening she looked like the artist who'd made the haunting paintings. Nick drove from Princeton and walked slowly around the gallery, seeing her at the center of accomplishment. Years later he will hang in his L.A. apartment her painting called "The Picnic," that large canvas with a solitary woman sitting at a table with a bowl containing one large strawberry.

When I dated my arrival in Rhinebeck, I described moving upstate in 1994 instead of 1992. Losing those years was a touch of amnesia that often accompanies big shifts, irreversible events. The cheeky, rash decision to give up the familiar had followed many years of staying put, the kind of stationary life that comes with agoraphobia. I had struggled out of the illness the way a swimmer thrashes for the water's surface, but unlike the swimmer who has only seconds, it had taken me nine years to get in the clear. In the years after Eckart had come out and left for his new life, I didn't have the confidence to reclaim my career as a journalist. I could only manage our neighborhood and so banded with a small group of folks selling real estate while waiting for their breaks as dancers, musicians, and film editors.

When the market was down in 1987, my penthouse apartment became more than the booby prize for the collapsed marriage. It was the only security I had. Without the confidence to resume writing for magazines, the maintenance plus a mortgage was unmanageable on child support and no alimony. Not demanding alimony had been part of my ongoing fantasy that the marriage might magically be saved. But this did not mean I would act swiftly. I was loyal to my habit of *seeing* and *not seeing,* as if all of life was to be questioned in the Talmudic tradition I had no claim to, having been raised in Greenwich Village by non-believers, first-generation Jews who had ironed themselves out, leaving no traces of immigrant beginnings. The actual sale of the penthouse and subsequent closing-date minuet suited my ambivalence: I could behave as if this wasn't really happening and that the rental I needed would magically appear, despite the teensy fact that I had four animals, three dogs and an ancient cat. The third dog had made us a pack that April evening when I'd walked Josie the doxie and Willie the terrier and discovered Nellie (as she would become) in the moonlight, tied to a fire hydrant.

Bridie, one of the neighborhood ladies still living in rent control, was spooning cat food onto a newspaper for the small white apparition whose face was hidden by its bangs. Even in daylight it wouldn't be possible to have known the puppy was a Bearded Collie and would weigh sixty-five pounds as a grown-up. Bridie recognized me in the lamp light and motioned me across the street. "Doooo something," she crooned in her long-held Irish brogue. (I would later report to my horrified friends, "I told her I could only take the pup for the night.")

The next morning another neighborhood woman heard, through the dog rescue grapevine, that a home was needed for the dazzling, glamour puppy. As soon as the woman took her, my palms became clammy, and a familiar lightheadedness told me I was near panic. This creature who had only spent the night with us was not supposed to leave. A week later, despite having named her Nellie, the woman brought her back where she belonged. Having sold the penthouse, I really needed a New York real estate miracle. Would my last year of rescuing and placing seven dogs in the Heights bring me a bit of rescue in the form of a landlord willing to rent to all of us—three dogs and an ancient cat?

As it happened, a cheerful and somewhat batty Italian longshoreman, who kept his own pigeons on the roof of his brownstone said, "Dogs? Who cares how many? Just be clean and pay on time. You got the dogs I got the birds. They call me Dr. Doolittle."

I was going back to the old neighborhood, not of my childhood but of Nico's. It was a holding pattern and was all that I could manage.

For someone so opinionated, I was hopelessly indecisive. Back and forth I went, contemplating the city or the "country" although Nellie had tipped the balance. I had to admit that three dogs and a cat should be leading me to the country. But after nearly two years of maneuvering Josie, Willie, and Nellie down the stoop and around the block, approaching the end of my IRS capital gains deadline, I was still waffling, unable to leave and restless, but attached to what had always been home. I would keep looking at places.

I made an appointment to see a small brownstone that needed work. On a Sunday afternoon I took the dogs out before heading over to meet the realtor. As we turned the corner of Clinton Street, a large white janitor's Clorox vat flew through the air and splat open a few feet from the four of us. It took seconds to realize it had come from above, not from the sky, but from the top-floor window where a man in an undershirt was shouting. Without hesitation, I called out, "You can't do that! That's dangerous!" What was I thinking? Was I observing my little boy's class at Montessori? Calling out the thug in the undershirt?

"Son of a bitch! I'll show you dangerous!" In a flash, he appeared on the stoop, brandishing a bottle which he then smashed against the railing, "I'll get those dogs! I'll get you!"

Three days later I was met at the Rhinebeck train station by my college roommate, Sybil, who'd brought Bea to the hospital after my Caesarean and who'd left Brooklyn the year before. When I started to waffle about the one sweet house in the village that could meet the IRS capital-gains deadline and that I could afford to renovate, she said, "This is IT, definitely IT."

Before I could make the move upstate, I had to make a stop at Lenox Hill hospital for an unnecessary complete hysterectomy. If the surgery's assault on tissue and muscle weren't so literal, it would have been a perfect metaphor for what I was feeling about moving. Now, a bit torn apart myself, I was striking the set in Brooklyn and setting out for the prim little village of Rhinebeck. The Greenwich Village kid was finally getting her picket fence, the one she had invented when she edited her childhood.

It became crucial to have a fence installed before arriving with the three dogs. Why I couldn't have walked them for a week or so on their leashes was a mystery. Did I want that moment, as soon as we'd arrived, of leading them through the house to the kitchen door, which I opened, clapping my hands and shouting, "Okay, go!" They flew across the sodden March grass. Willie headed for the north corner, which would be his favorite place for ten years. The girls sniffed, staying closer to the house. Tusie the cat, who'd been born in our Second Place backyard, never could climb that fence but was back on grass, after years on the penthouse rooftop.

In those first months, punctuated with weekly trips to see my ailing but not docile mother, I continued to feel split and not wholly anywhere although the train ride up the Hudson was always hypnotic. On one of those return trips, after visiting her in the ICU at New York Hospital, I watched the sun sliding behind the mountains and thought for an instant... my mother is dying not soon but right *now*.

Two hours later, as I walked into the house, the phone was ringing. Trying to quiet the welcoming dogs, I asked the doctor to repeat, "A procedure failed. Your mother has no pulse." She died on my father's birthday. He'd come to celebrate with me and instead of letting me get a dog sitter for the day had insisted on staying with them, not accompanying me, not going anywhere near her. That evening we had dinner at the Inn, as he wished. The next day when I wanted to return to say goodbye he didn't offer to come with me; instead, reminded me I'd just seen her. At seventy-nine he was as mysterious as ever.

Was he still furious with her or was his childhood fear of disease and death still calling his shots, as it had when his brother was dying of cancer and he moved us across the country to North Hollywood? Was he still giving me wrong advice as he had when he told me not to tell any boyfriend about her illness? Was the artist who created exquisite watercolors (landscapes, cityscapes, never portraits) still unable to show up—to be wise instead of brusque and dismissive—to finally give me the right advice?

I found myself grieving in a town where I had one dear friend and just the start of other connections. I was hesitant to burden new people with old information that would have framed the way I was experiencing my mother's death not with relief but with searing regret for not telling her I'd stopped blaming her for what she'd been given, when she could still hear it. I choose to call her Mother, not Bea, in my recollections... wild as wind and wrapped in wildflowers, giving the blooms to my Mother not to my Grandmother who bit her. I could now return to that mischievous, small girl running wildly around the Bleecker Street garden, in the Village, as my Mother held out a sweater, insisting on protection from the evening chill. I'm giggling as I tease her, proud of my speed and happy to be fooling around with my Mom.

I continued to take from the album what I needed—my mother and me side by side at Loews' Egyptian palace, on Greenwich Avenue, entranced with Betty Grable on the Technicolor screen, my mother dressing up in my Dad's pajamas to amuse, to comfort me when he was in L.A. for those months designing camouflage for the war effort, my mother when her spunk to defy my father by bringing home the Christmas tree was spunk and not words that could fly like bullets.

I was getting the picture of what it means to be familiar and known and how that is distinct from being new in town. The famous grayness of winter in the Hudson Valley closed in on the village, on my huge backyard banked with snow. For someone who'd essentially been married to her house (the way agoraphobics attach), it was strange not to have a favorite room in the new place. But the dogs had their favorite couch in the little library, and so I settled mostly where they rested. That small front parlor would become a place of sadness and comfort that first winter.

If winter is too close to death for some of us, my mother's death that November etched the bare trees and stony skies into me. There were none of the distractions of the city and too few people to help me through. The sighs of the dogs as they stretched out, helped make the unfamiliar house friendly, until we lost power because of a storm. Then where the hell was the doorman!? My adrenaline raced as it had when the man in the undershirt broke the beer bottle against the ironwork.

Mike, the collector who rode the village garbage truck every Tuesday, asked me why I looked so sad and, and as the truck pulled away, called out, "You'll see her again. I promise."

As homesick as I was, I knew this village web would somehow begin to comfort me, if I gave in. I also knew enough not to tell Mike I didn't believe in what he had no doubts about.

Eckart had observed in rare moments of ironic affection that I didn't rush things that I took my time even if the building was burning. Ever so slowly I stepped out of mourning and began to make friends. The middle of winter forced the car issue. Once it was mine, sitting in the driveway like a little gray coffee pot, I began to use it. I'd had a license that I'd gotten, never intending to drive. When I confessed to the counselor I was seeing for grief therapy that I was too afraid to take the car out of the village, she advised me to put Nellie in the back seat. Her large white face would be in the mirror and would keep me company, she assured me. And so with my extravagantly beautiful Scottish sheep dog keeping me safe, I learned to move around the county.

When I could drive, I returned to working in real estate. While I memorized the back roads I was moving mostly on automatic pilot, separated from what I remembered as my real, city self: the woman who had props, longtime residency, friends, and the assumption of a writing life even if the novel didn't get born but didn't die. Now transplanted to Rhinebeck, I couldn't settle into any kind of writing routine. I was too absorbed with distinguishing between loneliness and solitude to consistently show up to work. I wasn't rushing it.

If regret is the thief in the night that robs you of the juice that creates change, that thief was a constant visitor. The flame was turned way down, and I was simply grateful for a growing circle of pals, the soft light in my little house and my dog family who filled the place left by Nick, now in Hollywood. It seemed a writing life would continue to elude me or, more truthfully, that I would keep fencing with it.

The years took my creature kids: Tusie's ashes were scattered under the Rose of Sharon to remember her birth in our Brooklyn garden, Josie's went under the forsythia outside the kitchen window and Willie's were buried in the back of the yard where he'd spent his last years patrolling and bothering the squirrels. Nellie, the youngest, got to become a literary dog, after all, when I finally joined a writer's workshop. She greeted the other three women with that human smile of hers, settled onto her pillow, and was never even restless as we nipped and tucked one another's paragraphs late into the night. I had found myself in a safe place—to write, to percolate—to rewrite. None of this had happened on home ground or, as I used to think of New York as the scene of the crime. I was working, at last, ninety miles north of the city in a house I thought of as The Dog House, where three creatures tumbled around with me in their midst and fulfilled the contract dogs make with us: to be forever kids. Without their company I would not have left New York. The three of them had led me up the Hudson.

When I attended a dinner party the conversation turned to how we'd found our way to the Valley. I was asked, "Where did you grow up?" I was tempted to reply "In Rhinebeck" but knew it would provoke more questions than I was up for that evening. If driving lends itself to metaphor, learning to drive had been the first signal that I might grow up—Upstate. The Village and the Valley was where I had, indeed, grown myself up, on good days, and most of the time.

LAST WORD

Nick, called from his car to tell me he's racing up the 405, from his office in Los Angeles to a hospital in Ventura, to be with his father, who was on life support. The staff at his assisted-living facility couldn't find the "Do Not Resuscitate" document allowing him to die from a natural cause, from the heart attack that deprived his brain of oxygen for 30 minutes. Nick's been on the phone with the E.R. doctor, urging him to remove the breathing tube his father never wanted. They remove it.

Although I haven't lived with Eckart for 30 years, I've been his second medical advocate for more than a year, ostensibly to help Nick, who lived 90 miles away, and also for reasons I haven't wanted to look at. I hesitated before asking, "Do you want me to meet you there?"

When we entered the small room off the E.R., Nick went quickly to his father, touched his hair and his warm cheek, and put his hands on Eckart's chest under the blanket. I won't know Nick held his hands until later when he tells me that he wanted to feel their strength one more time. Eckart had spent his last year in a wheelchair, becoming weaker each month but managing, until recently, to hide the dementia that had begun years before. Although I have put my hands on my euthanized animals, my fear of dead humans kept me from touching my former husband's face. I can only touch the blanket and say,

"What a complicated fellow you were." I was saying it for my son as well as for myself.

We spent nearly an hour in the small room with Nick signing papers, a social worker kindly offering sympathy, and the young doctor who had disconnected the breathing tube, after locating the D.N.R. document, assuring us that Eckart would have been brain-dead. A risk-taker from his childhood in Germany, he'd exited as speedily as he'd driven—first the Autobahn, then American highways. Now he'd had what the Germans call *eine schoenest Tod* (a beautiful death). A once strikingly handsome man, he lay with his mouth wide open, his dentures left in his assisted-living studio apartment this one last time. I'd introduced myself as "Nick's mother" and sat off to the side. The social worker wanted me to know that there were bereavement support groups in the small town where I lived. But were they for former spouses? Did I qualify for support after 30 years of living apart? Can grief for loss be rekindled by final loss? Or is it grieving for the end of possibility, of revisiting the decision and asking him, "Did you ever regret leaving?" I realized I'd always been waiting for him to say about our twenty years together, "It wasn't nothing."

Despite my history with this man, the hurt, the fury, and the deep doubts he'd sown when he canceled twenty years of our life together, I didn't want to leave him there alone, to be wheeled away to a cold vault, pending more paperwork and cremation. I wanted us to sit with him, to be together as a family. I imagined that if we kept a vigil I might be able to touch his skin, then still warm, and for the first time be less afraid of death. For as his spouse, albeit former spouse,

I was next in line—or so it seemed there in the all too bright light, shimmering around me.

In the following weeks, after the scattering of his ashes, the "sea burial" as Eckart's brother called it, and the memorial luncheon which included just six of us, I was surprised to find myself back in the album I thought I'd left behind decades ago: Eckart had framed my youth and my motherhood and, most importantly, created protection from my mother. No longer in the foreground of each other's lives, we remained in each other's background for years, never as out of touch as others who divorce. It wasn't *nothing* even in separation.

Although I'd recovered from the agoraphobic years and resumed freelance editing, I was to discover that humiliating mid-life dating was too risky for a phobic who didn't know how to drop the storyline, didn't know how to live in the present tense. When I was asked why I had never remarried or re-coupled, I would say crisply, "I'm cured," when really I was in retreat, with Tusie and my pack: Willy, Josie, and Nelly.

It's taken too many more years to finally admit that Eckart wasn't the cause of my solitary life after the marriage but, just as I'd allowed my ill mother to seduce and reject me, seeing myself as a reflection in Eckart's eyes was a learned habit, as familiar as seeking the mother who had gone missing when psychotic bipolar illness became her new normal. Agoraphobia was not only a place to park fear and rage: it made me her daughter. And as so many of us do, I choose to marry the absentee parent, a man elusive from the start, before finally admitting to being closeted. Even if I had no control over the end of the marriage, I did have some choice in how to respond, how to prevail and to flourish. For even as we suffer, energies we can't anticipate are at work, and a moment can still take our breath away.

www.ingramcontent.com/pod-product-compliance
Lightning Source LLC
Chambersburg PA
CBHW070910120626
46546CB00001B/212